WILLIAM BLAKE
TIRIEL

WILLIAM BLAKE
TIRIEL

FACSIMILE AND TRANSCRIPT OF
THE MANUSCRIPT
REPRODUCTION OF THE DRAWINGS
AND A
COMMENTARY ON THE POEM

BY

G. E. BENTLEY, Jr.

OXFORD
AT THE CLARENDON PRESS
1967

Oxford University Press, Ely House, London W. 1

GLASGOW NEW YORK TORONTO MELBOURNE WELLINGTON
CAPE TOWN SALISBURY IBADAN NAIROBI LUSAKA ADDIS ABABA
BOMBAY CALCUTTA MADRAS KARACHI LAHORE DACCA
KUALA LUMPUR HONG KONG TOKYO

PREFACE

THE purpose of this work is to present the text and designs of Blake's *Tiriel* so that they illuminate one another in a way that has not been possible since the manuscript was separated from the drawings early in the nineteenth century. Only one of the *Tiriel* drawings has ever been reproduced with a transcript of the poem before, and five of the designs given here have not been reproduced at all. Similarly, though the manuscript has been repeatedly transcribed, it has never previously been reproduced.

With these reproductions are a transcript of the poem and a study of the illuminated Prophecy. In particular, the study systematically examines the significance of the *Tiriel* designs in a way that has never been attempted before.

The publication of this book completes the reproduction of Blake's narrative poems with their designs. Except for the *Tiriel* drawings not yet traced, students now have access to all the materials necessary for conclusions about the poem.

The editor is deeply grateful to the following owners for their generous permission to reproduce their *Tiriel* drawings:

Gwen Lady Melchett (nos. 1, 6)
The Syndics of the Fitzwilliam Museum (no. 2)
The Trustees of the British Museum (no. 4)
The Victoria and Albert Museum, Crown Copyright (no. 7)
Sir Geoffrey Keynes (nos. 8, 11)
Mrs. Louise Y. Kain (no. 10)

The Trustees of the British Museum also gave permission to reproduce the manuscript of *Tiriel*.

Photographs of the *Tiriel* drawings were supplied by the British Museum (nos. 1, 4, 10, 12), Cambridge University Library (nos. 8, 11), the Fitzwilliam Museum (no. 2), A. C. Cooper Ltd., London (no. 6), and the Victoria and Albert Museum (no. 7).

G. E. B.

October 1964

CONTENTS

TABLE OF REPRODUCTIONS

INTRODUCTION

Tiriel has always proved a puzzle to commentators on Blake. The printed prophecies are difficult enough, but an unfinished manuscript like this one aggravates the problems. The very words Blake wrote in *Tiriel* are sometimes difficult to read; Swinburne read 'Mnetha' as 'Mutha',[1] and no one is quite sure what the original name of Hela was ('Hala'? 'Hili'?). The names that appear in the poem are unfamiliar ones which seem to derive from the most diverse sources, while the narrative can only be pieced together from chance allusions, some of them now deleted. Consequently the adventurous critic would do well to work his way cautiously into the woods, taking frequent compass bearings, and regularly pausing to assess his progress and his resources.

Let us first establish who the characters are and what relationship they bear to one another. The multiplication of such names as Heva, Zazel, and Ijim seems much less perverse when we perceive their clear blood relationship and the significance suggested by the probable sources of their names.

All the characters mentioned in *Tiriel* are members of one enormous family:

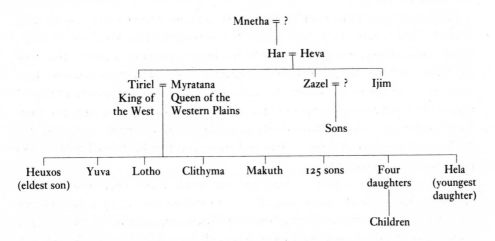

The relationships between the members of the earliest generations are the most obscure. Mnetha, a protective nurse-figure, is probably the progenitor of all the

---

[1] Algernon Charles Swinburne, *William Blake* (London, 1868), p. 199 fn.

rest, for Har twice speaks of her as 'my mother Mnetha' (ll. 75, 78). It is, of course, true that Har is presented as senile in the text (though not in the drawings), and this might be merely his trusting, infantile way of referring to his nurse. However, since Mnetha's role *is* motherly, we might do well to accept that she is in fact Har's 'mother'. Certainly no other clear indication of his parentage is given.

Har and Heva are referred to as 'The aged father & mother' (l. 63), and Heva 'took old Tiriel in her mothers arms' (l. 91). The implication that Heva is Tiriel's mother is made clearer by Hela, who tells Tiriel that Har and Heva forget 'the offences of their most rebellious children Or else thou wouldest not have livd' (ll. 304-5). In her senility, Heva does not recognize Tiriel—she says to Tiriel, 'Thou art my Tiriels old father' (l. 93), and a couple of lines later she identifies 'my Tiriels old father' as 'old Tiriel'—but we have no good reason to disbelieve Hela. Since Heva is self-contradictory, and the implications of what Hela says are clear, we may be fairly confident that Har and Heva are Tiriel's parents.

Tiriel twice speaks of his 'brother Ijim' (ll. 163, 173), and Zazel identifies himself to Tiriel as 'thy brother Zazel' (l. 335). These three are the only offspring of Har and Heva in the poem. Ijim does not appear to have had children, but Zazel's sons are mentioned (ll. 35, 329).

Tiriel says, 'I am Tiriel King of the west' (l. 354), and Mnetha agrees to the title: 'I know Tiriel is king of the west' (l. 72). It is noteworthy that Tiriel still 'is king', in the present tense, though like Lear he has lost the panoply of power. (His wife Myratana was 'once the Queen of all the western plains' [l. 3], but the past tense here seems to derive not so much from her lack of power as from her imminent death.) Since only Tiriel among the sons of Har and Heva is spoken of as a king, and since Tiriel's eldest son is shown in the drawings as a king, it is reasonable to suppose that King Tiriel was the eldest son of Har and Heva, and that he derived his kingship partly from his primogeniture.

Tiriel and Myratana seem to have had one hundred and thirty sons and five daughters. When Tiriel's curse took effect, 'an hundred men' (l. 271), all evidently sons of Tiriel, were killed, and only 'thirty of Tiriels sons remain' (l. 276), though Tiriel swore that the curse should 'clean devour all those guilty sons' (l. 281). He also has 'five daughters' (l. 260), who in turn have 'children' (l. 275). Only five of the sons and one of the daughters are named in the poem.

Among these children, the first is Heuxos, who seems to be 'the eldest son of

Tiriel' (l. 12) and Myratana (l. 25), who 'raisd his mighty voice' (l. 12) against Tiriel and defended his brethren when Tiriel appeared with the dying Myratana in his arms and denounced them. He also acts with authority when he orders 'a son of Zazel to dig their mother a grave' (l. 35). In the seventh drawing the crowned figure is almost certainly Heuxos. It is natural to find that Heuxos derives his authority from his position as eldest born and king.

The brothers of Heuxos are only named incidentally. Tiriel says that the dying Myratana no longer 'groans . . . at the birth of Heuxos or Yuva' (l. 25). Since Heuxos is 'the eldest son', the order in which Heuxos and Yuva are named may indicate that Yuva was the second born. In a deleted passage Ijim identifies three other 'sons of Tiriel' (l. 216) as 'Lotho Clithyma Makuth' (l. 225). The only one of these who appears in a passage which Blake allowed to stand is Lotho (see l. 197). In the first drawing one of Tiriel's sons is crowned with bay leaves and another with vine leaves, and their houses with 'lofty towers' (l. 256) are 'richly-sculptured' (Design 9). This symbolism may imply that Tiriel's sons represent the arts. Only four or five of the sons are shown in the drawings, and it is difficult to connect clearly any of the brothers depicted with any of those named in the poem besides Heuxos.

Tiriel speaks of 'Hela my youngest daughter' (l. 266). She says she was born Tiriel's 'slave' (l. 291). Since Tiriel's sons, and presumably his daughters too, had been enslaved by Tiriel (l. 17) some seven years before (ll. 41, 167-8, 335), and since Tiriel's sons 'rebeld' (l. 17) and freed themselves some two years later (ll. 285-8), it is possible to deduce that, if we are to understand these terms literally, Hela was between six and seven years old during the action of the poem. It is clear that such terms as 'slave' and 'year' are to be taken metaphorically throughout the poem. Nevertheless, it may not be far-fetched to conclude that Hela was born during the period when Tiriel held his children in slavery.

The qualities of some of these named characters are made clearer by references in the poem and by the apparent sources of the names. Probably the simplest deriva-tions are those of Har and Heva, who are represented in the text as timorous and senile, playing with birds and running for protection to Mnetha. The identification of their peaceful valley as a kind of Eden is reinforced by the derivation of their names. Heva seems to be a form of Eve, which is Eva in Latin and Havvah in Hebrew. A Latin or Hebrew Bible, or an ordinary English Bible with learned annotations, could have taken Blake to these forms of the name. The word Har means mountain in Hebrew, as Blake could have discovered from similar sources, or from Jacob

Bryant whose book he probably illustrated;[1] it appears as a proper name of a place ('Hara') in 1 Chronicles v. 26. This identification is supported by the references to 'the mountains of Har' (l. 345) and 'the vales of Har' (l. 56, repeated in *The Book of Thel*, Plate 4). 'Har' is actually described as a wise king (as Blake's Har evidently once was) among the Scandinavians in Mallet's *Northern Antiquities*, a book with which it is very likely Blake was familiar.[2]

Har is mentioned in a passing reference in *Thel*, of about the same date as *Tiriel* (1789), and Har and Heva both appear once in a rather puzzling context in *The Song of Los* (1795), where 'all the sons of Har' seem to represent 'The human race'. In that poem 'Eternity was obliterated & erased' evidently on

> that dread day when Har and Heva fle*d*
> Because their brethren & sisters liv'd in War & Lust:
> And as they fled they shrunk
> Into two narrow doleful forms:
> Creeping in reptile flesh upon
> The bosom of the ground:
> And all the vast of Nature shrunk
> Before their shrunken eyes.
>
> Thus the terrible race of Los & Enitharmon gave
> Laws & Religions to the sons of Har binding them more
> And more to Earth: closing and restraining:
> Till a Philosophy of Five Senses was complete[;]
> Urizen wept & gave it into the hands of Newton & Locke[.]

At the bottom of the page are represented a couple, whom from the text we should identify as Har and Heva, fleeing in terror, but they are youthful and bear no clear resemblance to any of the figures in the *Tiriel* designs.

Much of this description in *The Song of Los* seems consonant with *Tiriel*, for there Har and Heva 'were as the shadow of Har' (l. 59), and Blake might equally well have written in *Tiriel* that 'all the vast of Nature shrunk Before their shrunken eyes'. Similarly, 'the sons of Har' represent mankind in both poems, and it was the 'Philosophy of Five Senses', called 'Laws' in *The Song of Los* and *Tiriel* (l. 358), which corrupted them. The association of Urizen in *The Song of Los* with Tiriel in the poem

---

[1] Jacob Bryant, *A New System, or, an Analysis of Ancient Mythology* (London, 1774), vol. i, p. 94: 'Har and Hor signify a mountain'.

[2] Paul Henri Mallet, *Northern Antiquities* [tr. John Calder, ed. Thomas Percy] (London, 1770), vol. i, p. 8. According to *Icelandic Poetry, or The Edda of Saemund*, tr. A. S. Cottle (London and Bristol, 1797), p. 73 fn., Harr is a name for the god Odin.

that bears his name as the lawful corrupter of mankind is also useful and illuminating, for Urizen is of course Blake's principal symbol of cold, worldly rationalism. There are, however, some important inconsistencies. There is no evidence in *Tiriel* that 'Har and Heva fled', as they did in *The Song of Los*, and in *Tiriel* it seems more likely that they stayed in the valley of Har when their sons left them (l. 128). Further, *Tiriel* contains no allusion to 'their brethren & sisters', and in *Tiriel* the 'War & Lust' we hear of appear to come after, rather than before, the senility of Har and Heva.¹ Parts of the context in which Har and Heva appear in *The Song of Los* are so alien to *Tiriel* that it would be unwise to place weight upon any but the most obvious similarities in the two poems.

Tiriel's five daughters have often been associated with the five senses, largely on the grounds that the number five appears in each group. The daughters are not significantly differentiated from each other in the drawings, and it would be danger- ous to push this association. It is common to identify Hela, the only daughter named, with the sense of touch,² but this is largely a derivation from Blake's later writings, where the sense of touch is the last avenue to eternity to be closed. Since blind Tiriel chooses Hela specifically to be his guide, it would seem more natural to associate her with sight, if she is to be linked to one of the senses.

It is significant that Hela leads Tiriel to his death, or at least to the place where he dies, for Mallet frequently uses her name as synonymous with death, and in a note to 'The Descent of Odin' Gray called her 'HELA, the Goddess of Death'.³ Mallet describes her in some detail:

[*In*] a place consisting of nine worlds, reserved for those that died of disease or old age HELA or death . . . exercised her despotic power; her palace was ANGUISH; her table was FAMINE; her waiters were EXPECTATION and DELAY; the threshold of her door, was PRECI- PICE; her bed was LEANNESS: she was livid and ghastly pale; and her very looks inspired horror.⁴

The fair young Hela depicted in *Tiriel* as a powerless though defiant slave clearly bears but a distant relationship to her grim Teutonic namesake.

It happens that we know more about Hela than we do about most of the originals of Blake's prophetic names. With others of these prototypes, as with Hela, it becomes

---

¹ Har is merely mentioned, along with Ijim, among the 'myriads' of 'Sons of Los & Enithar- mon' on *Vala*, p. 115. No other figures named in *Tiriel* appear in any other work by Blake.

² S. Foster Damon, *William Blake, His Philo- sophy and Symbols* (Boston and New York, 1924),

p. 72; Northrop Frye, *Fearful Symmetry* (Prince- ton, 1947), p. 245; D. V. Erdman, *Blake Prophet against Empire* (Princeton, 1954), p. 121.

³ *Poems by Mr. Gray* (London, 1776), p. 105.

⁴ P. H. Mallet, *Northern Antiquities* (London, 1770), vol. i, p. 121.

apparent that Blake intended to import only a few of the original associations of the name into his poem. He was clearly widely read in occult literature and in alien mythologies, but the mysterious and divine attributes of the names which he adapted were regularly transformed almost completely when they entered Blake's poems.

Tiriel, the blind king whose only power lies in his terrible curses, and his brother Zazel, driven out to cower in caves, appear to come, directly or indirectly, from Cornelius Agrippa's *Three Books of Occult Philosophy* (1651), where 'Tiriel [*is*] The Intelligence of *Mercury*' and 'Zazel The spirit of *Saturn*'.[1] The identity of the names makes it more likely that Blake had picked up the word 'Tiriel' from an occult source than that it is an adaptation of blind 'Tiresias', of 'Tiria', the Hebrew word for fear,[2] of 'ritual',[3] or of 'reality'.[4] The value of most such anagrammatic derivations lies in their mnemonic use to the reader rather than in what they tell us of Blake's intentions. Tiriel in Blake's poem is associated, it is true, with some of the qualities of his occult prototype, such as wisdom and intelligence, but these qualities we learn from the poem, not the source.

It has been supposed that 'Mnetha . . . is a Blakean transmogrification of Athena, goddess of Reason',[5] but, while it is true that she is a wise protectress to Har and Heva, it is unlikely that her name itself was very directly modelled on Athena's. The syllable 'Mne', so difficult in English (and so improbable when it appears by itself as an adjective in *Thel*, 'Mne Seraphim'), is fairly clearly derived from the Greek root meaning memory. Unlike so many derivations of Blake names from Greek roots, this one can be shown to have been known to Blake. In his 1809 *Descriptive Catalogue* he wrote that 'The Greek Muses are daughters of Mnemosyne, or Memory', and in his manuscript 'Vision of the Last Judgment' he came closer to the present point when he asserted:

Jupiter usurped the Throne of his Father Saturn & brought on an Iron Age & Begot on Mnemosyne or Memory The Greek Muses which are not Inspiration as the Bible is. Reality was Forgot & the Vanities of Time & Space only Remembered & Calld Reality[.][6]

---

[1] Cornelius Agrippa, *Three Books of Occult Philosophy*, tr. J. F. (London, 1651), p. 243. Tiriel is listed with some new attributes (the number four, Michael, the spirit Cochabiel, with Daleth, and the signification wisdom) in [Jacques] Basnage, *History of the Jews*, tr. Tho. Taylor (London, 1708), p. x. The name Tiriel occurs, after the time of Blake's *Tiriel*, in *The Conjuror's Magazine*, i (October 1791), 80 (with Zazel and Bne Seraphim), and in Francis Barrett, *The Magus; or Celestial Intelligencer* (London, 1801), p. 147.

[2] H. A. Hewlett, 'Imperfect Genius: William Blake', *Contemporary Review*, xxviii (1876), 779.

[3] Mark Schorer, *William Blake* (New York, 1946), p. 227.

[4] Margaret Rudd, *Divided Image* (London, 1953), p. 92.

[5] S. Foster Damon, *William Blake, His Philosophy and Symbols* (Boston and New York, 1924), p. 72.

[6] Notebook, p. 71.

Mnetha is clearly, in the context of *Tiriel*, memory and conventional wisdom, and her charges Har and Heva have nothing of Inspiration about them; they have forgotten reality and remember only 'the Vanities of Time & Space'. The association of her name with the Greek word for memory is a useful mnemonic aid in interpreting the poem.[1]

The only other name in *Tiriel* which has been reliably traced is Ijim, which is translated in the King James Bible as 'satyrs' (Isaiah xiii. 21).[2] Blake might have found the name in an old or an annotated Bible, but he is more likely to have discovered it in Swedenborg's *True Christian Religion* (1781), where the Ijim are described in a wild context very similar to that in *Tiriel*. Swedenborg explains that the Ijim represent 'diabolical Love', or

the Love of Self, which is indeed called Love, but . . . its true Nature, is Hatred; for it loveth none out of or beside Itself; . . . its inmost Affection is a continual Lust to rule over all and to possess the Property of all, and at last to be worshipped as a God . . . . various Lusts thereof appear in Hell, at a Distance, like various Kinds of wild Beasts; some like Foxes and Leopards; some like Wolves and Tygers; and some like Crocodiles and venemous Serpents; . . . the Desearts where they live consist solely of huge Heaps of Stone, or of barren Sand, with Bogs interspersed, full of croaking Frogs; . . . dismal Birds fly, and make a mournful Screeking over their miserable Abodes. These are the Ochim, Tziim, and Jiim [*misprint for* Ijim] mentioned in the Prophecies of the Old Testament, where their Love of Dominion arising from the Love of Self is spoken of. See Isaiah xiii 21. Jerem. i. 39. Psalm lxxiv. 15.[3]

These visions of 'Leopards . . . Tygers . . . venemous Serpents . . . Heaps of Stone . . . croaking Frogs' are very like the phantoms of the 'lion . . . tyger . . . bright serpent . . . toad . . . rock' (ll. 202-12) which torment Blake's Ijim.

As far as we can discover the mythological antecedents of Blake's names in *Tiriel*, then, they come from the Bible (Har, Heva), Agrippa, Swedenborg, the occult (Tiriel, Zazel, Ijim), and legends of Scandinavia (Hela) and Greece (Mnetha). The range and obscurity of the sources are striking, and the symbolical level of the poem

---

[1] Dylan Thomas uses the same name in 'Before I Knocked' (*Collected Poems 1934-1952* [London, 1952], p. 7), which begins:

> Before I knocked and flesh let enter,
> With liquid hands tapped on the womb,
> I who was shapeless as the water
> That shaped the Jordan near my home
> Was brother to Mnetha's daughter
> And sister to the fathering worm.

Thomas's source and intention here are obscure to me.

[2] This and the Swedenborg reference following were pointed out by Northrop Frye, *Fearful Symmetry* (Princeton, 1947), pp. 242-3.

[3] Emanuel Swedenborg, *True Christian Religion*, tr. John Clowes (London, 1781), pp. 65-66.

is emphasized by realization of its materials, but Blake used so few of the associations of the names as he found them that rarely can we learn much on the narrative level from their origins.

One difficulty in interpreting *Tiriel* lies in the elementary obscurity of the action, both before the scene opens and after the actors arrive on stage. It may be well, then, to summarize what happens in the poem.

Before the poem begins, in the remote past, Har's sons Tiriel, Ijim, Zazel, and perhaps others, left Har (l. 128) and his Eden in the East, probably to found kingdoms of their own. For a time they lived in harmony with one another, evidently in Tiriel's 'once delightful palace' (l. 5), where they loved one another—or at least Ijim 'once lovd Tiriel' (l. 188).

The first action of importance for the narrative apparently took place *seven* years before the scene opens, when Tiriel last saw Ijim in the palace (ll. 167-8). It was evidently then that Tiriel 'enslavd the sons of Zazel' (l. 41) and 'chaind' Zazel (l. 335). Probably at the same time Tiriel enslaved his own sons (l. 17). (He may have tried to enslave Ijim too, but Ijim proved invulnerable and escaped to wander wild in the forests.) Tiriel wanted to establish the blessing (l. 18) of law (ll. 358, 360), but his sons, compelled to live by the law, found 'His blessing was a cruel curse' (l. 18), for, as Blake wrote elsewhere, 'One Law for the Lion & Ox is Oppression'.[1] It was *seven years* before the action of the poem begins (l. 168) that Zazel and his sons cursed Tiriel (l. 41), presumably at the time they were enslaved. When we first see Tiriel he seems to have been blind for some time; perhaps he was blinded by Zazel's curse.

It must have been *two years later* that Tiriel's sons 'rebeld' (l. 17) and freed themselves. (They may have kept Zazel's sons as their own slaves, for one 'son of Zazel' seems to be in a menial position to them [l. 35].) They did not leave Tiriel (ll. 130-1); instead they stayed in their houses with the 'lofty towers' (l. 256) near the palace, and apparently they offered to allow Tiriel to remain with them. Tiriel bitterly refused the 'charity' of his sons (ll. 37-38). He said that they had 'smitten' him (l. 165), and Ijim believes that they turned Tiriel out 'To be the sport of wintry winds' (l. 236), though the sons said that Tiriel himself had chosen to wander (l. 39).

For *five years* Tiriel dwelt with his wife Myratana 'in the desolate rock', waiting for his sons to be destroyed by nature, by lightning, or by a tidal wave (ll. 285-7). *At the end of the five years*, Tiriel proclaims that 'all the time of grace is past' (l. 268), and, as the narrative begins, he returns to the palace with the dying Myratana.

---

[1] *The Marriage of Heaven and Hell*, Plate 24; compare l. 360 in *Tiriel*: 'Why is one law given to the lion & the patient Ox'.

With Myratana in his arms, Tiriel confronts and threatens his sons (ll. 1-10), who in turn defy him (ll. 11-19): 'His blessing was a cruel curse. His curse may be a blessing[.]' Myratana dies in Tiriel's arms, and only then does Tiriel damn his sons for ruthlessness to Myratana (ll. 19-33), though this curse seems to have no effect. Tiriel prepares to bury her by the palace as part of his malediction ('Curse on your ruthless heads, for I will bury her even here' [ll. 33-35]), but his sons offer to bury her for him (ll. 36-42), and he acquiesces with an execration (ll. 43-51): 'Bury your mother but you cannot bury the curse of Tiriel'.

Turning from them, Tiriel 'Wanderd till he that leadeth all led him to the vales of Har' (ll. 52-56), where he finds Mnetha with Har and Heva, who are 'like two children . . . Playing with flowers & running after birds' (ll. 57-61). They do not recognize him, and run from him in fright to Mnetha, though Tiriel protests his peaceful intentions (ll. 62-67). They do not believe him when he calls himself 'Tiriel', so he dissembles and asks for mercy as a nameless 'harmless man' (ll. 68-83). Har is disarmed by Tiriel's helplessness, so like his own, and welcomes him to share their peaceful, strifeless Eden (ll. 84-97). Mnetha presses him for an account of himself, presuming that he, like all known men, is related to them ('Why shouldest thou conceal thyself from those of thine own flesh' [ll. 98-99]), and Tiriel astonishes them by telling them, falsely, that he is father of a northern race destroyed for its wickedness (ll. 100-5). Mnetha can scarcely believe that there exist 'More human creatures on this earth beside the sons of Har' (ll. 106-7), and Tiriel comforts her by saying that he is the only survivor of the other race (ll. 108-9). They then all sit and eat, and Har blesses Tiriel's 'piteous face', at which Tiriel is much moved (ll. 110-18). Har and Heva are amazed when Tiriel says he cannot stay with them ('I am forcd to wander'), and they try vainly to tempt him with their innocent pleasures, with singing songs and gathering cherries (ll. 119-42). At last Har says with unintended and prophetic irony, 'If thou dost go . . . I wish thine eyes may see thy folly' (l. 127). Even Mnetha joins in their entreaties (ll. 143-5), but at her interference Tiriel alters his request to a 'command', and they tremblingly allow him to go his way (ll. 146-52).

On his blind journey, Tiriel meets Ijim in the forest, who taunts him with being the 'tempter of dark Ijim', now reduced to 'the last of thy deceits' (ll. 153-61). Tiriel recognizes that he is helpless before his mighty brother, and asks for mercy (ll. 162-8), but Ijim persists in his delusion that Tiriel is only posing as Tiriel, and takes him 'like a slave' (l. 177) to the western palace to confront him with the true Tiriel (ll. 169-94). When he finally bears Tiriel to the palace, the sons see him come in horror, apparently because 'They knew twas vain to strive with Ijim' (ll. 195-200).

Ijim boasts of his prize, and asks for the real Tiriel, and Tiriel ironically seconds him (ll. 201–24), but when Ijim is disillusioned he merely releases Tiriel and wanders forth disconsolately to his 'secret forests' (ll. 225–42).

When Tiriel confronts his sons, no longer restrained by the mercifulness of Myratana or the invulnerable power of Ijim, he pronounces a magnificent curse upon his sons—'Thunder & fire & pestilence, hear you not Tiriels curse'—which is immediately carried out in the deaths of 'an hundred men ... The four daughters ... And all the children' (ll. 243–77). Tiriel chooses out 'Hela my youngest daughter' (l. 266) to lead him forth; 'Now Hela I can go with pleasure & dwell with Har & Heva' (l. 280). Hela goes with him unwillingly, protesting at his cruelty (ll. 278–92), and Tiriel threatens her with 'a terrible fathers curse' unless she obey him lovingly (ll. 293–9). When she defies him (ll. 300–16), he curses her as well (ll. 317–20), and 'snakes infolded round Her madding brows' (ll. 321–2). It is significant that, while Tiriel rejoiced in the destruction of his sons, 'her shrieks appalld the soul of Tiriel' (ll. 322–6).

Hela leads him past the caves of Zazel, where Zazel taunts them (ll. 327–41), but Tiriel merely meekly 'smote his breast & trembling passed on'. When 'The howling maiden' and her father come to the Valley of Har, Mnetha greets them fiercely with a warning (ll. 342–52), but when Tiriel identifies himself as 'King of the west' she leads them to Har's tent (ll. 353–6). Tiriel apparently bows before his father (he 'felt the ankles of aged Har' [l. 356]), and in an extraordinarily eloquent speech of self-recognition he catalogues his errors (ll. 356–91). But though it may be a speech of confession, it scarcely ends in repentance, for his last words 'Return ... a curse on thee O Har'. His words end with his life, and 'He ceast outstretchd at Har & Hevas feet in awful death' (l. 393).

Few systematic hints are given in the narrative of the location and significance of the places visited in this blind odyssey, but there are enough references to establish the chief polarity between Tiriel's palace in the West and the Valley of Har in the East.

Tiriel's 'beautiful' (l. 1), 'once delightful palace' (l. 5) has 'Gates' (l. 1) and a 'wide court' (l. 253) in the text, though not in the drawings. Near the palace live his sons, who speak of 'our houses' (l. 38) which have 'lofty towers' (l. 256), and, in the designs (no. 9), richly sculptured columns. The palace is clearly in the West, for Tiriel is 'king of all the west' (l. 70), and when he went from the Valley of Har towards his own palace he was 'Westwardly journeying' (l. 183).

At the other geographical extreme are 'the vales of Har' (l. 56) a day's journey to the

East, which are bordered on their western side (l. 62) by the 'pleasant' 'lower garden' (l. 351) and, a little further West, by 'the mountains of Har' (l. 345). In 'the valley of Har' (l. 68) are the 'happy tents' (l. 345) of Har, Heva, and Mnetha, and 'the cage of Har' (l. 124).

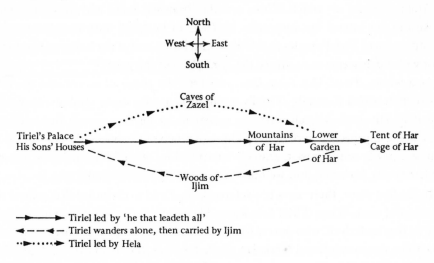

Two other literal places are mentioned vaguely in the poem. The first is Ijim's 'secret forests' (l. 242) from which he came 'down' to meet Tiriel (l. 155), and the second is 'the caves of Zazel' (l. 328). Tiriel passes near the first when journeying westward from the Valley of Har to his palace, and he and Hela approach the latter *en route* from the palace to the Valley of Har. It is tempting to speculate that 'the caves of Zazel' are in the north, as are those of Winter in 'To Winter' (*Poetical Sketches*), and Ijim's woods in the south, but Blake made no effort in the poem to round off his geographical symbolism as neatly as this.

There are four other metaphorical references to places which seem not to be correlated with other sites in the poem. Tiriel threatens his sons with 'northern fogs' (l. 44) and with 'buriers . . . from the east' (l. 49), and Ijim cries that 'Tiriels house' 'is as false [*as*] Math*a* & as dark as vacant Orcus' (l. 239). 'Matha' seems to be merely a play upon 'Matter', and 'Orcus' is the Latin word for Hell. None of these metaphorical places is referred to elsewhere in the poem or in Blake's other writings, and in their context they seem rather incidental.

The first design shows, in the background of Tiriel's palace, a pyramid beyond a meandering river, and the implication is very strong that the scene is Egypt. In the text the Valley of Har, with its garden and tents, and the peaceful, pastoral existence of Har, Heva, and Mnetha have strong overtones of Eden before the Fall, and the fact that geographically the Valley of Har is East of Tiriel's palace in Egypt would reinforce this conclusion. Perhaps the mountain that borders Har's Eden is related to Mount Pisgah, on which Moses saw the Promised Land and died. Obviously Blake did not intend his geography in *Tiriel* to be taken very literally, but the identification of Tiriel's realm in the West with Egypt and of the Valley of Har in the East with Eden seems to reinforce the symbolism of the poem.

As a whole, *Tiriel*, like *King Lear*, concerns the abuse of power and the self-destruction which it entails. Tiriel's wanderings are far more symbolic than real, and it is only with his self-torturing questions in his last speech that ordinary existence is approached very nearly. Through much of the poem Tiriel seems to be almost a power unto himself, scarcely controlled by others. His authority has important limits, however, and we must remember what these limits are.

In the first place, there are a few references in *Tiriel* to divinities that control the destinies of men. When Tiriel first leaves his palace alone after Myratana's death, it is 'he that leadeth all' who directs him to the Valley of Har (l. 56). This sounds very much like the conventional Christian simile for God, the 'God ever nigh' of 'The Little Boy Found' in *Songs of Innocence*. When Tiriel returns to his palace, we do not know the agency that guides him until Ijim captures him, but after the cursing of his sons Tiriel needs his daughter to lead him away. His only scatheless journey is the one he makes under the guidance of 'he that leadeth all', before he has rejected the hospitality of Har and Heva or cursed his children.

Tiriel himself is evidently aware of this force above men, for in a deleted passage he says, 'God bless my benefactors' (l. 137; cf. ll. 87–88), and he feels that he himself acts under divine compulsion: 'long I staid not at his palace for I am forcd to wander' (l. 121). This force is evidently understood by Tiriel and his children to be very like an impersonal worldly fate, with few moral attributes. Tiriel did not oppose the invulnerable strength of Ijim because 'He knew . . . Ijims words were as the voice of Fate' (l. 179), and his sons cry despairingly when Ijim confronts them with Tiriel: 'O we are but the slaves of Fortune' (l. 229). Hela says her father is 'Leagued with evil spirits' (l. 290), and the deluded Ijim sees 'fiends' all round him (l. 240).

In the second place, Tiriel's remaining power, so far as we see it exercised, is circumscribed as to object and circumstance. When his sons rebelled Tiriel and Myratana waited five years 'for the fire to fall from heaven' on his children (ll. 285–6), but while Myratana is alive Tiriel does not call the curse down on the children himself. She is somehow a restraining influence on him; as Tiriel explains to Hela, 'now my wife is dead & all the time of grace is past You see the parents curse' (ll. 288-9). Further, Tiriel's power is evidently limited to 'the parents curse'; he can enslave his sons and plant serpents in Hela's hair, but he is powerless to resist Ijim (despite his vain threat of a curse [l. 166]), and when Zazel mocked him and 'threw dirt after them' Tiriel merely 'trembling passed on' (ll. 341, 340). His last words indicate vividly the limit of his power; he curses Har, but himself dies 'at Har & Hevas feet' (l. 393). He can destroy his offspring and himself, but not others.

Analogues for the actions have confidently been discovered in a great variety of sources, but none offer very extensive similarities. The most obvious parallels are those in the metaphors of *King Lear*. Tiriel's repeated identification of his offspring with 'Serpents' (ll. 22, 215, 309) reminds us immediately of Lear's anguished 'How sharper than a serpent's tooth it is To have a thankless child' (I. iv. 310-11). Like Lear, Tiriel is guided in his distress by his youngest daughter, who he mistakenly thinks 'laughs at affection[,] glories in rebellio*n*, scoffs at Love' (l. 295; cf. III. iv. 14-16). Both Tiriel and Lear are turned out by their children, they think, to wander wild in nature (ll. 39, 236; II. iv. 210-14) where they can 'not sleep nor rest because of madness & dismay' (l. 139; III. ii. 1-60), and in their outrage and madness they call upon the thunder to destroy their children (ll. 243-55; II. iv. 164-70). Perhaps the most direct echo is when the senile Har asks Tiriel in his trouble: 'My sons have left me[;] did thine leave thee' (l. 128), and we recall Lear in his madness asking of Mad Tom, 'What, have his daughters brought him to this pass?' (III. iv. 66). Such parallels, however, are chiefly confined to imagery. It would be an extraordinary author who could construct a story round a father driven to madness by his children and not echo *King Lear*.

Elaborate attempts have been made to link *Tiriel* to the history of George III[1] and to Sophocles' *Oedipus at Colonus*,[2] but the similarities, like those to *Lear*, seem somewhat superficial. Tiriel is, like George III, King of the West and mad, but Tiriel's kingdom is much more of Biblical Egypt than of contemporary America, and Tiriel's wanderings in exile, which after all take up the whole of the poem, are difficult to reconcile with revolutionary history. On a similar plane, blind Oedipus led by his daughter to the place where he finds his death is much like Tiriel, but this action occurs only in the last third of *Tiriel*, and the difference between the loving Antigone and the loathing Hela is surely crucial. As with *Lear*, Blake may have

[1] D. V. Erdman, *Blake Prophet against Empire* (Princeton, 1954), pp. 122-4.

[2] Kathleen Raine, 'Some Sources of *Tiriel*', *Huntington Library Quarterly*, xxi (1957), 5-13.

incorporated symbolic elements from the history of his own time and from *Oedipus at Colonus* into *Tiriel*, but neither played a dominant or clear part.

It is tempting to try to illuminate Blake's more difficult works from passages elsewhere in his writings which seem easier to grasp. In particular, one wonders whether his great construct of the Four Zoas, developed much later, can be applied to *Tiriel*. There are a number of indications that Blake may have been working out the implications of his system in *Tiriel*, as he had been in the addresses to the seasons in *Poetical Sketches*. As with the Prophecies up to *The Four Zoas*, the polarity in *Tiriel* is chiefly twofold rather than fourfold, between a rational power in the West and an imaginative one in the East. As Tiriel is similar to Urizen and Har to a senile Los, so the physically tremendous Ijim may be likened to Tharmas, the senses, and the enslaved Zazel to Luvah, the emotions. As in the later myth, the actors in *Tiriel* once lived together in harmony, but when they are led from their Eden by the reasonable Tiriel they war among themselves and degenerate further and further. Not only is Tiriel's realm physically discrete from those of Har, Zazel, and Ijim, but even foolish Zazel keeps carefully to his own caves, and does not trespass upon 'the wood', Ijim's realm, 'where wild beasts resort' (ll. 341–4). The chief difficulty with such parallels is that in *Tiriel* these actors never were equal (as they are in the later myth), for Zazel, Tiriel, and Ijim all appear to be the sons of Har. As sons, they should share his powers, instead of representing, as they seem to, qualities quite different from his. The Four Zoas may be latent in *Tiriel*, but clearly at this early date Blake was still groping toward his final formulation of the relationship of the powers in the universe.

The most tantalizing analogue with *Tiriel* I have noticed is in the story of Joseph in Genesis. We know that Blake was actively interested in the story of Joseph not long before the time when he was probably composing *Tiriel*. For *The Protestants Family Bible* of about 1781 he engraved a plate after Rubens of 'Joseph sold to the Ishmeelites', and for *The Exhibition of the Royal Academy* in 1785 he made drawings of 'Joseph's brethren bowing before him', 'Joseph ordering Simeon to be bound', and 'Joseph making himself known to his brethren'.[1] These, of course, are the chief points of Joseph's story: his sale by his jealous brothers into Egypt (Genesis xxxvii. 28), his rise to power under Pharaoh after prophesying seven years of plenty and seven of famine, the arrival of his brothers to buy corn after two years of famine, when they 'bowed down themselves before him' (Genesis xlii. 6), Joseph's ruse when he 'took from them Simeon, and bound him' (Genesis xlii. 24) in order to persuade his father and all his brothers to come to Egypt, and their return

---

[1] All three drawings are now in the Fitzwilliam Museum.

to Egypt, when 'Joseph made himself known unto his brethren' (Genesis xlv. 1). The points of similarity between this story and *Tiriel* are few but they are striking. Like Joseph and his brethren, Tiriel and his brothers evidently originally came out of the East to found a kingdom in the West, which the first *Tiriel* design shows with an Egyptian pyramid. Like Tiriel's sons, Joseph's brethren became virtual slaves, for as 'Joseph said unto the people, Behold, I have bought you this day and your land for Pharaoh' (Genesis xlvii. 23). In both cases, the tyrant's motive is benevolence to his subjects, to protect them from nature and from themselves. After two years of Tiriel's tyranny his sons abandon Tiriel's law; after two years of the famine Joseph prophesied, his brothers submitted themselves to Egypt. When Pharaoh would not let the children of Joseph leave Egypt, Moses' God cursed Egypt with successive plagues of blood, frogs, lice, flies, murrains, boils, thunder, hail and fire, locusts, 'thick darkness', and the death 'of all the firstborn in the land of Egypt'.[1] When Tiriel returned from the Valley of Har to find his sons still in his palace with its Egyptian pyramid, he cursed them with 'Thunder & fire & pestilence' (l. 255) and 'thick darkness' (l. 270); 'And all the children in their beds were cut off in one night' (l. 275). Like Moses, Tiriel comes to the very threshold of the Promised Land before he dies.

These parallels are inconsistent and unsatisfactory, but they do seem striking. Here as elsewhere, however, Blake seems to have been taking over details and metaphors rather than a whole story.

Madness characterizes the actions of all the principal characters in the poem. It seems reasonable to suppose that once they were sane, if they lived in harmony with Har, or perhaps when they lived lovingly in Tiriel's palace. As we see them, however, Har, Tiriel, Ijim, and Zazel are all mad in different ways. Old 'foolish' Zazel and his sons live like savages, on roots and water, in caves, and when their tormentor came near them they 'threw dirt after' him in futile rage (ll. 329–41). Ijim is a mighty wild man living in forests and tormented by visions of lions, tigers, serpents, toads, newts, rocks, shrubs, rivers, and lightning, against which he struggles madly (ll. 202–12). He sees 'fiends' around him (l. 240), but though he sees terrors everywhere, he and Tiriel are 'Blind to the pleasures of the sight & deaf to warbling birds' (l. 181). Because it terrifies him, Ijim struggles blindly against nature. Har and Heva are senile and helpless, 'like frighted infants' (l. 64), now 'delighted with infant dreams' (l. 61), now 'trembling like infants' (l. 71). They are dependent for all their knowledge upon Mnetha, and in the text even she is 'now aged' (l. 58). Tiriel, like Ijim,

---

[1] Exodus vii. 20; viii. 6, 17, 24; ix. 6, 10, 24; x. 14, 22; xii. 29.

deliberately chooses to wander in the wilderness, refusing the 'charity' of his sons (l. 37). Like Ijim he struggles madly against his environment, though his environment is not nature but society. As Hela says, he is a cruel destroyer and consumer (l. 300), and Tiriel recognizes that 'Madness & deep dismay possess the heart of the blind man' (l. 147; cf. l. 139).

Tiriel's sons, however, are not conspicuously mad; they are the only ones who live in anything like a community and show any capacity for acting together. Tiriel's mad destructiveness, his rage against all round him, and his compulsion to curse them, commence, so far as we can tell, only after he has left his palace. There appears to be a direct connexion between harmony in Tiriel's palace and madness for those who wander outside it. This is consonant with Blake's later myth, in which madness and self-destruction result from the disruption of the primordial harmony.

Har and Heva, whose names are Hebrew and Latin for Mountain and Eve, seem to be man's first parents, Adam and Eve. They believe that all mankind is descended from them (ll. 106-7), and they live in a peaceful 'garden' (l. 351) with tame, harmless animals, like an Eden before the Fall. They are degenerated from apparent former wisdom and strength, for they are now weak (l. 101), the shadows of their former selves (l. 59). They are 'waited on' by Mnetha (l. 58), to whom they run 'for refuge' (l. 64) when they are frightened. If, as the probable derivation of her name suggests, Mnetha represents memory, they are flying from the contemplation of present ills to the memory of past felicity. They are clearly unable to cope with their environment; they have no imagination and are governed by the remembrance of past hopes and fears. The inference often drawn that they represent Poetry and Painting, now degenerate through dependence upon mechanical memory, is by no means clear from the poem, but it is a fair extension of Blake's meaning in *Tiriel* in the light of his later ideas.

Har apparently represents a system of passive benevolence based on an innocent world of loving which does not account for, and therefore cannot cope with, natural evil. He and Heva 'are holy & forgiving[,] filld with loving mercy Forgetting the offences of their most rebellious children' (ll. 303-4), and Har assumes that all men, being his sons, are formed alike. He has formed 'laws' (l. 358) based upon this innocent misunderstanding of creation; he has worshipped his 'God of Love' and evidently tried to legislate 'heavens of joy' (l. 359) on earth. Such a misunderstanding of the universe is self-corrupting, and Har has degenerated until he is only fit to live in the world he has created. He has become what he conceived, which is only a fragment of total human capacity.

Tiriel identifies himself with the world Har had created in his own image. 'Thy laws O Har & Tiriels wisdom' apparently work toward the same end, and they 'end together in a curse' (l. 358). Tiriel has tried to form mankind in the image he conceives, but he finds that he must curb and destroy part of the child to make this possible:

> The child springs from the womb. The father ready stands to form
> The infant head while the mother idle plays with her dog on her couch[.]
> The young bosom is cold for lack of mothers nourishment & milk
> Is cut off from the weeping mouth with difficulty & pain[.]
> The little lids are lifted & the little nostrils opend[.]
> The father forms a whip to rouze the sluggish senses to act
> And scourges off all youthful fancies from the newborn man . . .
> And when the drone has reached his crawling length
> Black berries appear that poison all around him. Such was Tiriel[.]
>
> (ll. 375-85)

In the process of curbing the 'youthful fancies' Tiriel himself degenerates; he is

> Compelld to pray repugnant & to handle the immortal spirit
> Till I am subtil as a serpent in a paradise
> Consuming all both flowers & fruits & insects & warbling birds
> And now my paradise is falln . . . .
>
> (ll. 387-90)

His 'eloquent tongue' (l. 189) has been converted to a 'tongue of terrible curses' (l. 316), and he has learnt at the expense of his own destruction 'that men cannot be formed all alike' (l. 361). He has become blind to all aspects of reality save those which he himself has exalted; in carrying out his inhuman laws he has become a personification of blind justice. He has destroyed parts of himself, and by implication he has destroyed the sense of 'grace' in himself with the death of Myratana.

Tiriel learns with despair that his sons and all mankind are 'lawless' (l. 392), that all are formed differently, that no law can adequately govern all men. When he returns from the wilderness to his sons, at the beginning of the poem, he is hopeless, and when he leaves them he is flying 'far from hence' (l. 74) 'oer rocks & mountains' (l. 138), not *to* any specific goal. He deliberately 'seeks the woods' (l. 148), perhaps, as Hela later did, 'Hoping to end [*his*] life' 'where wild beasts resort' (ll. 343, 342). When he sees the peaceful harmony of Har and Heva, however, he is evidently roused to indignant rage at what he thinks is the rebellious, unnatural anarchy of his sons, and he returns and destroys them. When he curses them he destroys himself, as he himself recognizes:

> . . . now my paradise is falln & a drear sandy plain
> Returns my thirsty hissings in a curse on thee O Har
> Mistaken father of a lawless race my voice is past[.]
>
> (ll. 390–2)

Tiriel is destroyed by the law he created and cannot live by.

It seems possible that Tiriel's sons have found the harmony he could not achieve. Tiriel's severely classical palace is 'beautiful' (l. 1) in a mechanical fashion, with unornamented columns and, in the background, an Egyptian pyramid. Some years earlier Blake had engraved a design by Stothard for Bonnycastle's *Introduction to Mensuration, and Practical Geometry* (1782), in which he showed children playing with cubes and cylinders and pyramids like the fragments of classical buildings, and many years later he wrote on his Laocoön plate: 'The Gods of Greece & Egypt were Mathematical Diagrams'. It may not be fanciful to see a deliberate contrast between the description of the palace as 'beautiful' and as 'once delightful' (ll. 1, 5), for as he corrupted himself Tiriel may have altered his palace from one of eternal delight to one of cold beauty. It was also years later when Blake wrote that 'Grecian is Mathematic Form: Gothic is Living Form',[1] but he may have believed it when he wrote *Tiriel*. Certainly it seems significant that Tiriel's house is so severe and restrained, while the houses of his sons, as seen in Design 9, seem to be exuberantly sculptured. Further, two of his sons are crowned with the bay leaves of poetry and the vine leaves of enjoyment. Tiriel's art, like his laws, seems to represent the purely intellectual, while his rebellious sons, unconfined and living in harmony among themselves, may represent the whole man. If this is so, the tone of *Tiriel* is an extraordinarily tragic one, for Har, Heva, Ijim, and Zazel live primitively and degenerately, while Tiriel's curse will 'clean devour all those guilty sons' (l. 281), and Tiriel himself is parched and consumed by the curse. The curse of One Law for the Lion and Ox destroys not only those who live by that law but also those who defy it. *Tiriel* shows no middle way between innocence and experience, no escape for impulsive innocence. Blake's view of the world was seldom shown darker than it is in the tortured rhetoric of *Tiriel*.

---

[1] 'On Homers Poetry [*and*] On Virgil.'

Significance of the Drawings

The *Tiriel* drawings that have been traced fall into two clearly distinct categories. The first category is of those drawings which are obviously and closely related to some action of the poem (nos. 1, 4, 6, 7, 8, 10, 12). For instance, the text says that 'the aged man raisd up his right hand to the heavens[;] His left supported Myratana shrinking in pangs of death' (ll. 19-20), and the first design shows a blind man raising his right hand and holding up with his left a woman whose eyes are half-closed. In the text 'Har arose & laid his hand upon old Tiriels head' (l. 86), and the fourth design represents an old man standing with his hands on the head of the blind man shown in the first design, who kneels before him. According to the manuscript, Tiriel's 'five daughters . . . caught him by the garments' (ll. 261-2), and the eighth design depicts five women clutching the blind man's robe. These actions described in the text are so explicitly shown in the drawings that we can be confident that these seven drawing at least were made to illuminate *Tiriel*.

Further, the characterization in the designs is quite consistent. In nos. 1, 4, 6, 7, 8, 10, and 12 Tiriel is shown as a blind old man, bald except for a fringe of white hair at the ear-line, with a white beard, and a long-sleeved, unbelted, loose-fitting gown that reaches to his ankles. Har in the second, fourth, sixth, and eleventh designs is an old man of about the same apparent age as Tiriel, with a smooth, trouble-free face, and very long, silvery hair and beard, though with no marks of intelligence. In Designs 1, 7, and 8 one of the sons addressed by Tiriel, probably Heuxos, has a fair curling beard, and wears a strange, spiked crown, a wrist-length dark gown, and a pale mantle. Since these and other figures are recognizably the same in different designs, and since Har, Tiriel, or Heuxos appear in every one of the designs traced, we may have considerable confidence that all twelve designs belong to the same series, and that the series illustrates *Tiriel*.

Before going on to examine the consistency of text and designs, it will be well to record a number of anomalies. Most of the anomalies concern discrepancies between text and design, and some are fairly minor. The text, for instance, mentions Tiriel's 'grey hairs' (l. 14) and 'grey beard' (l. 196), but the designs show both Tiriel and Har with hair and beards of conspicuous whiteness. Similarly, Har says that Tiriel's beard is 'shriveld' (l. 88), but this is true only by comparison with Har's majestic beard which 'doth cover all my breast' (l. 114). Tiriel's beard is shown to be full but cut straight across the bottom. In the poem there are frequent references to the countless wrinkles of Tiriel's face (ll. 14, 88, 93, 115, 135, 315, 334), but these wrinkles are not conspicuous in the designs. The few lines shown on his forehead might easily be accounted for by the temporary concentration required of a blind man instead of by extreme old age. Har says to Tiriel, 'Thou hast no teeth old man' (l. 89), but the designs do not show Tiriel with the fallen cheeks of toothlessness. The text emphasizes the physical degeneracy of Tiriel and the intellectual degeneracy of Har, but the designs do not echo these contrasts. All these difficulties are relatively unimportant, and all might be accounted for by an artist's natural desire to depict his characters as beautifully as possible, even though this might involve him in defiance of his text.

Heva and Mnetha present a curious and rather special problem. In the text they are said to be 'aged' (ll. 58, 63), but in the second and eleventh drawings they are represented as beautiful young women with clear foreheads, smooth necks, and firm breasts. They look much alike here, with the same clear, symmetrical faces, and with similar waist length, pale hair parted in the middle. Mnetha's nose is perhaps a trifle straighter and longer than Heva's, and her mouth somewhat smaller. They are differentiated from each other, and identified, chiefly by their actions. However, not only do their appearances in nos. 2 and 11 seem to contradict the text, but in no. 4, and apparently in no. 3, they are depicted quite differently. They both look decades younger than Har in nos. 2 and 11, but in nos. 4 and 6 (and probably in the untraced no. 3 as well) Heva's costume and the lines of anxiety in her face make her seem more nearly Har's contemporary, and Mnetha's costume changes from one of classical simplicity to one in a rather fussy contemporary fashion. It is difficult to reconcile the flowing youth and beauty of Mnetha in nos. 2 and 11 with the prim, aunt-like figure in no. 4. Perhaps the explanation is that in nos. 2 and 11 Har, Heva, and Mnetha are alone, natural, and free, while in nos. 3, 4, and 6 they are with Tiriel, and are frightened, inhibited, and conventional.

Some of the drawings present other difficulties more basic to an understanding of the illuminated poem. Whereas Designs 1, 6, 7, 8, 10, and 12 quite clearly illustrate actions of the poem, nos. 2, 5, and 11 represent Har, Heva, and Mnetha in scenes which are not described, and which are scarcely alluded to, in the narrative. The second design shows Har and Heva bathing, and the fifth represents them 'playing Harps', but the text comes no closer to these actions than to say that 'Playing . . . they spent the day' (l. 60), or that they had 'many songs to sing' (l. 123). Har and Heva are once or twice described as sleeping (ll. 61, 347), as they are shown in the eleventh drawing, but the text certainly gives no prominence to the action. It is tempting to speculate that these designs illustrate lost lines of the poem, but the manuscript gives no indications that any leaves are lost, and on many pages it would have been easy to add a number of lines. Since Har is recognizably the same figure in the scenes which clearly come from the narrative (nos. 4 and 6) and in those which do not (nos. 2, 11), we must conclude that all these designs were intended to 'illustrate' the poem, though the word 'illustration' seems to have a meaning in Designs 1, 6, 7, 8, 10, and 12 different from that in nos. 2, 5, and 11.

It is striking that, whereas in the text Har is strictly secondary to Tiriel whenever he is seen, and appears in only about a third of the poem (ll. 57–152, 347–93), he is shown in fully half the drawings (nos. 2–6, 11). Further, when Har is depicted, not only is Tiriel, the protagonist, often excluded from the drawing (nos. 2, 3, 5, 11), but the relationship of the drawing to the text is often obscure (no. 3) or all but invisible (nos. 2, 5, 11). Evidently Har was more interesting to Blake graphically than literally. As he demonstrated in the *Songs of Innocence and of Experience*, Blake found it easiest to depict innocence and to describe experience.

Conceivably Blake was deliberately adding to his poem, by way of illustrations, incidents, and allusions that he did not choose to put in the text. Or perhaps the scenes of Har and Heva bathing and playing harps figured either in a draft of the poem now lost (though this seems somewhat unlikely) or in a version of the poem never committed to paper. If, for instance, Blake made the drawings first and composed the text later, the words as they were committed to paper might conceivably have taken on a life and direction of their own not entirely in accord with his original conception.

It seems to me most likely, however, that Blake never intended or attempted to 'illustrate' his own poem in the conventional sense, in the way that his friend Stothard made illustrations, for instance, or in the way that Blake himself later illustrated Hayley's *Ballads*. That is, he did not normally try to make a drawing slavishly represent in pictorial terms exactly what the passage expressed in words. To a man with Blake's unfailingly vivid imagination this would have smacked of redundancy. He evidently had the faculty of visualizing whatever he conceived or read to an extraordinary degree, and of transforming the literal facts into imaginative truth. He himself explained how this faculty works better than anyone else can:

[']What['] it will be Questiond [']When the Sun rises do you not See a round Disk of fire somewhat like a Guinea[?'] O no no I See an Innumerable company of the Heavenly host crying [']Holy Holy Holy is the Lord God Almighty[.'] I question not my Corporeal or Vegetative Eye any more than I would Question a Window concerning a Sight[.] I look thro it & not with it[.][1]

[1] Notebook, p. 95.

Clearly, to a man with such a highly developed faculty of visualization, the mechanical translation of words into pictures would have been tedious, journeyman work scarcely requiring imagination. Blake was capable of such work, but he was not much interested in it. He could copy a picture faithfully on copper if necessary, as he did all his life to earn his bread, and he could mechanically echo words in designs, as he did in Mary Wollstonecraft's *Original Stories* (1791) and in Hayley's *Ballads* (1802, 1805), but such tasks apparently did not stimulate his imagination very much. What he liked best, what he did most successfully, was to depict not the literal scenes but the metaphorical and spiritual implications of the text. In later years, when he came to make designs for Young's *Night Thoughts* (1795-7), Gray's *Poems* (1804?), Blair's *Grave* (1805-6), Milton's *Paradise Lost* (1807-8), *The Book of Job* (1815-26), and Dante's *Divine Comedy* (1824-7), he consistently took great liberties with the text, adding and translating details almost at will, or rather at imagination, correcting and supplementing his author as he thought necessary.

Similarly, in illustrating his own work after *Tiriel*, Blake regularly expanded the implications of his text and multiplied the details of his own narrative. Thus in 'The Little Girl Lost' from *Songs of Innocence and of Experience* the 'Little Girl' of the title is 'Seven summers old' in the text, but in the illustration she is two or three times that age, and in the embrace of a naked young man. In the same way, the 'Preludium' of *Europe* is entirely devoted to the eternal lament of 'The nameless shadowy female', but the design shows a naked assassin with a dagger lurking in the rocks for a laden traveller who is approaching. Neither of these scenes could have been deduced from the text, though they are fairly clear, if remote, implications of the poems. All his life it was Blake's habit to use his designs to comment on his texts, to amplify the actions, to translate the implications of the narrative into new, pictorial metaphors. Consequently it is dangerous to use the word 'illustration' in connexion with Blake, for his designs rarely 'illustrate' a work in the ordinary sense of the word. Blake himself spoke of his 'Illuminated Books',[1] and it is always safest to use the less precise word 'illumination' in connexion with Blake's work rather than 'illustration'.

Probably the difficulty we have in interpreting the relationship between Blake's text and designs is that we normally expect the words to precede and govern the designs. By mentally reversing this process, we can also grasp without difficulty the situation where designs govern text, as they do for instance in Hogarth's 'Rake's Progress'. We are, however, ordinarily unprepared for such a complex inter-

[1] Prospectus 'To the Public', 10 Oct. 1793.

relationship as exists between Blake's words and designs, in which each illuminates and supplements the other.

Blake's *Tiriel* designs seem to represent an early stage in his technique of illuminating literary works. Some of the drawings (nos. 1, 4, 6, 7, 8, 10, and 12) represent a very specific action of the narrative quite clearly, but in each case details of the designs significantly expand the implications of the poem. In the first, seventh, and eighth designs Heuxos is shown in the forefront of the sons of Tiriel as a crowned king, though in the text he is merely the eldest of the rebellious brothers. In the first design the Greek and Egyptian architecture and the bay and vine leaves in the hair of the sons may be seen as crucial aids in interpreting the poem, which could scarcely have been gleaned from the text itself. In the fourth design the extraordinarily conventional, nanny-like costume of Mnetha, and in the tenth design the Greek dress of Hela, exposing one breast, make explicit some implications of the text over which we might otherwise have hesitated. Tiriel is shown dead in the twelfth design, as described in the text, but he is not 'outstretchd at Har & Hevas feet', as in the text, but at the feet of Hela.

Some of the other drawings, nos. 3, 9, and 11, depict actions evidently of a fairly generalized kind which yet may be related to the poem by close reading. At least twice Har and Heva are spoken of as asleep, as they are shown in no. 11. In these cases, the difficulty is that the actions depicted are of no great importance in the text, and that they seem to omit details upon which the text does lay stress. For instance, in the poem Har and Heva are never mentioned except when Tiriel is present, but in the third design, where Har is talking to Mnetha, with Heva by his side, Tiriel does not seem to appear at all, though according to the poem he was a witness of the scene and indeed must have been the subject of what Har was saying. Similarly, in the ninth drawing, evidently Tiriel's sons are staring 'in awe at some . . . catastrophe', but, though the catastrophe is made explicit in the text, apparently the nature and cause of the catastrophe are invisible in the drawing. In terms of the narrative itself, it is surprising that Blake did not choose more dramatic scenes to represent in his drawings.

In the remaining drawings, nos. 2 and 5, the actions represented do not appear in the poem at all, and seem almost inconsequential so far as the narrative is concerned. It is only because Har is recognizably the same figure in the fourth design, which is closely connected with the narrative, and in the second (and apparently the untraced fifth) design that these drawings are associated with *Tiriel* at all; that and the fact that when the drawings first came to light in 1854 they were then in the same collection

and were thought to form part of the same series. The scenes of Har and Heva
bathing and playing harps can only be related to the poetic narrative metaphorically
rather than literally. In so far as they belong to the illuminated poem, they clearly
emphasize the peaceful innocence of Har and Heva's lives while the text emphasizes
their helpless senility. In the text Har and Heva are only seen with Tiriel, and, faced
with the power and bitter experience which he represents, they seem terribly vulner-
able. The illustrations of Har, Heva, and Mnetha show the blissful life of innocence,
a peaceful Paradise before the Serpent. Apparently life in the Valley of Har and
Heva was more important and attractive to Blake than he could easily show in the
poem alone. Here, in these designs of Har and Heva bathing and playing harps,
Blake is clearly emphasizing new aspects of his poem.

In the narrative, Tiriel lives in the rocks and goes to his palace twice, to the caves
of Zazel, to the woods of Ijim, and twice to the Valley of Har. The palace is the most
important place in the poem, but it appears in only three or four of the drawings
(nos. 1, 7–9). The Valley of Har, which is shown in seven drawings (nos. 2–6, 11, 12),
is clearly the most important place so far as the drawings are concerned. In 'reading'
the text and the series of designs together, the polarity of Tiriel's palace and the
Valley of Har is seen much more clearly than would have been possible in either text
or designs alone.

If the drawings were to be inserted into the poem approximately by the sections
of text they illustrate, they would be moderately well distributed through the poem.
They appear as follows:

Drawing number	MS. page	Lines
1	1	19–20
2	3 ?	59–60 ?
3	3	75, 84
4	4	86
5	5 ?	123 ?
6	6	149–51
7	8	192, 215, 233
8	10	261–2
9	10	271–7
10	12	321–2, 327
11	13 ?	347 ?
12	15	393

Drawings 2, 3, 4, and 8, 9 are rather too closely bunched by comparison with the others to have made it easy to include any intervening text in the published work, but it will be noticed that in each of these groups appears a drawing which has not been traced (nos. 3, 9). It is, of course, possible that when discovered these drawings will reveal details demonstrating that they refer to different incidents in the poem.

We can only guess what publication plans Blake had for his illuminated poem. He may have intended it to go no further than its present manuscript form. We have, however, no other finished and illuminated narrative poem which Blake did not evidently intend, at least at one time, for publication, and the relatively high finish of the designs makes us wonder whether he meant to publish *Tiriel*.

We can only speculate about the method of publication he may have intended. Apparently Blake did not make such highly finished drawings in preparation for the etching of his other Illuminated Works—or at least no sets of such drawings have survived—and in all his other etched works full-page designs alternate with smaller marginal designs of a kind not found in *Tiriel* at all. In his published narrative poems through 1794 Blake made his title-pages into full-page designs; normally he made a frontispiece as well; almost all the pages had designs at least of a marginal kind; and as time went by Blake interspersed more and more full-page plates through the text.

Designs in Narrative Poems

Title and date	Full-page plates (including title-page and frontispiece)	Pages with both design and text	Pages with no designs	Total pages
The Book of Thel (1789)	1	5	2	8
Visions of the Daughters of Albion (1793)	2	9	..	11
America (1793)	2	16	..	18
Europe (1794)	4	13	1	18
The First Book of Urizen (1794)	10	16	2	28

In none of these poems did Blake attempt to give graphic scenes from the text at regular intervals, as he seems to have done with *Tiriel*. In none of them are the designs anything like as elaborate and finished as they are in *Tiriel*. In none of them are there anything like as many large designs as Blake made for *Tiriel*, nor do the large designs illuminate anything like such a high proportion of the text. In short, these *Tiriel* designs differ in size, in relationship to text, in conventionality, in finish, and indeed in kind from those Blake made for his other works in Illuminated

Printing. Certainly the illuminations in *Tiriel* are unique among Blake's works in these respects.

It seems very unlikely that *Tiriel* can have been created with the idea of transferring it to copper in a form like that of Blake's other narrative poems. Perhaps the most striking difficulty in this respect would have been the very shape of the drawings. The *Tiriel* designs are all considerably wider than they are high, whereas the ordinary page, and every page Blake illuminated before about 1804, is of course higher than it is wide. This eccentric shape for the *Tiriel* designs would have meant that, if they were to be engraved on an ordinary page and near their present shape, they would have had to be put on sideways; the text would have read one way and the designs another. As users of this volume will perhaps testify, this is a troublesome and irritating arrangement.

These considerations suggest that the *Tiriel* designs were made before 1789, when Blake fairly launched his Illuminated Works with *Thel* and *Songs of Innocence*. The shape of the drawings would suggest as well that even conventional engravings, perhaps for publication with a text in ordinary typography, were not contemplated either. From both text and designs it may be inferred that *Tiriel* was Blake's earliest illuminated narrative and that from the beginning he never meant to publish it. Blake was rarely as concerned as we might wish with making his works public; a number of his best works never got past the manuscript stage, and it is reasonable to suppose that works of which we know nothing were lost. From the age of 14 on, Blake was writing poems for which he had no audience. *Tiriel* differs from these other unpublished works only in its finished designs. Perhaps *Tiriel* was Blake's earliest ambitious union of text and design; perhaps it was *Tiriel* which impelled Blake to create his method of Illuminated Printing in order to publish such works as *Tiriel*. By the time he had perfected his technique other more successful works, such as *Thel* and *Songs of Innocence*, may have occurred to him, which absorbed his attention to the exclusion of *Tiriel*.

History of the Drawings

No contemporary allusion to either the manuscript or the drawings of *Tiriel* has been traced. Both designs and manuscript probably stayed in Blake's possession until his death in 1827. After his death they presumably went with his other property to his widow Catherine. When she died in 1831, Blake's effects passed to Frederick Tatham, who sold the drawings gradually over the years as he found customers for them. One of these customers was the dealer Joseph Hogarth, who wrote that as 'Blake's executor' Tatham 'possessed several of his drawings, many of which I purchased from him'.[1] The earliest reference to the *Tiriel* designs is in the catalogue of Hogarth's sale at Southgate and Barrett's on 8 June 1854, where among Blake's watercolours is listed Lot 643, 'Twelve elaborate Subjects, designed to illustrate a Work, the subject unknown.' If we may trust this rather tenuous chain of evidence, the *Tiriel* drawings stayed in Blake's possession until his death, when they passed to his widow Catherine and thence to Frederick Tatham and Joseph Hogarth.

At the 1854 sale the twelve drawings realized £3 and passed into the possession of 'that distinguished Patron of Art, Elhanan Bicknell, Esq.', whose watercolours were sold after his death at Christie's on 1 May 1863. In the Christie catalogue they were described briefly and somewhat inaccurately as Lots 377–88. They were listed in order of subject, rather than of narrative, the drawings in which Har appears (nos. 3, 4, 11, 9, 2, 6, 5) preceding those centring on Tiriel (nos. 10, 8, 7, 1, 12). Har is described merely as an 'aged man' and Tiriel as a 'blind man', except that in nos. 1, 7, 8, and 12 Tiriel is misleadingly called merely 'the aged man'. The descriptions were reserved to the point of reticence. For instance, no. 10 was given as 'The blind man walking with a female', with no reference to the snakes in her hair. The prices ranged from 5s. for no. 9 to £2. 4s. for no. 1, and averaged a little better than 17s.

One of the people at the sale was W. M. Rossetti, who made more detailed and accurate notes on the drawings than were given in the Christie catalogue. These notes he printed in Gilchrist's *Life of William Blake* published that year. At the head of his description he wrote:

> This is a puzzling series—evidently a *series*; often very fine in invention and composition. There is a sort of rational, consecutive look about the subjects, which disposes one to believe that they illustrate some known story, rather than any invention of Blake's own: some of them, however, might do for his unpublished poem, 'Tiriel,' a piece of erratic Ossianism. Others suggest Ruth, Lot, Œdipus, Lear, Priam; but one fails in attempting to carry any of these histories on through the whole series. I follow the order of subjects as

[1] Wilfred Partington, 'Some Marginalia', *Times Literary Supplement*, 28 Jan. 1939, p. 64, quoting Hogarth's note dated '1877'. In his sale of 7 to 30 June 1854 mentioned below, Hogarth sold seventy-eight Blake pictures in Lots 237, 643, 1095, 1521, 1922, 2363, 2784, 3270, 3705, 4180, 4624, 5068, 5082, 5509, 7112, and 7553.

Hogarth had owned other Blake drawings as early as about 1843, when he sold some to Ruskin through George Richmond (*The Letters of John Ruskin*, ed. E. T. Cook and Alexander Wedderburn [London and New York, 1909], vol. i, pp. 32–33).

in the sale-catalogue, modifying some of the titles there given, with the view of bringing out the subjects more distinctly.[1]

Through Rossetti's catalogue description, and the revised version Rossetti prepared for the second edition of Gilchrist's *Life* in 1880,[2] most of the information available about the *Tiriel* drawings was transmitted. In 1863 the set of drawings was broken up, and most of the designs disappeared for some time. A few indeed have not been recorded since 1863.

Drawings Ownership

Drawing number	Owner
1	*Gwen Lady Melchett*, 4 Belgrave Square, London, S.W. 1, acquired through Agnew from the Christie sale of 19 May 1958, Lot 13.
2	*Fitzwilliam Museum*, Cambridge, England, acquired from Edward H. Marsh in 1953.
3	*Untraced since 1863*, when, according to the marked catalogue in the Rosenwald Collection of the Library of Congress, it was sold to 'Noseda[?]' for 9s.
4	*British Museum Department of Prints and Drawings*, acquired in 1913.
5	*Untraced since 1863*; no buyer is given in the Rosenwald copy of the catalogue, but the price is given there as 12s.
6	*Gwen Lady Melchett*, acquired through Agnew from the Sotheby sale of 15 June 1960, Lot 12.
7	*Victoria and Albert Museum Department of Prints and Drawings*, bought through E. Parsons at the D. J. Percy sale at Christie's, 15 April 1890, Lot 96.
8	*Sir Geoffrey Keynes*, Lammas House, Brinkley, Newmarket, Suffolk, acquired at Hodgson's in 1943.
9	*Untraced since 1863*, when it was sold to Hogarth for 5s.
10	*Mrs. Louise Y. Kain*, Louisville, Kentucky, acquired through Francis Edwards and Duschnes at the Christie sale of 19 May 1958, Lot 14.
11	*Sir Geoffrey Keynes*, acquired at Hodgson's in 1943.

[1] Alexander Gilchrist, *Life of William Blake*, '*Pictor Ignotus*' (London and Cambridge, 1863), vol. ii, p. 253. In the 1880 edition (vol. ii, p. 273) Rossetti repeated this tentative introduction, though by that time he had been persuaded by Swinburne that the drawings were indeed 'from Blake's poem "Tiriel" '.

[2] In the second edition (1880, vol. ii, p. 273) Rossetti rearranged the drawings approximately in the correct order (nos. 1, 3, 11, 2, 5, 4, 7, 8, 9, 10, 6, 12).

Drawing number	*Owner*

12   *Present owner untraced.* The drawing was exhibited at the British Museum Department of Prints and Drawings in 1957, along with nos. 1, 4, and 10, and photographs of all four drawings were made in the British Museum then. This design was sold at Christie's, 19 May 1958, Lot 15, to the dealer Jacob Schwartz, of 14 Chichester Terrace, Brighton. Unfortunately Mr. Schwartz cannot recall to whom he sold the drawing.

Only five of the designs appear to have been reproduced heretofore. They are:

Drawing number	*Where reproduced*

1   Martin Butlin, 'The Bicentenary of William Blake', *Burlington Magazine*, C (1958), 40-44.

2   Geoffrey Keynes, *A Bibliography of William Blake* (New York, 1921); Laurence Binyon, *The Drawings and Engravings of William Blake*, ed. Geoffrey Holme (London, 1922), Plate 4; *The Writings of William Blake*, ed. Geoffrey Keynes (London, 1925), vol. i, Plate 3; Darrell Figgis, *The Paintings of William Blake* (London, 1925), Plate 94; Thomas Wright, *The Life of William Blake* (Olney, 1929), vol. i, Plate 8; E. Marsh, *A Number of People*: A Book of Reminiscences (New York and London, 1939), 353; Sir John Squire, review of Sir Edward's reminiscences in *Illustrated London News*, CIV (8 April 1939), 596.

4   L. Binyon, *The Drawings and Engravings of William Blake* (1922), Plate 5; T. Wright, *The Life of William Blake* (1929), vol. i, Plate 8.

7   T. Wright, *The Life of William Blake* (1929), vol. i, Plate 9.

11   Geoffrey Keynes, *Bibliotheca Bibliographici* (London, 1964), Plate X.

Only one drawing has ever been reproduced with the text of *Tiriel* before, and no critic has ever considered the relationship of more than two or three of the designs to the poem.

Description of the Drawings

Drawing number 1 (Pl. I)

At the left Tiriel, in the ankle-length, unbelted, loose gown he wears throughout, holds the drooping Myratana with his left hand and gestures with his right hand toward three of his sons, one in a crown, dark gown, and mantle, one with bay leaves and a short gown, one naked except for a mantle. The text illustrated is certainly 'The aged man raisd up his right hand to the heavens[;] his left supported Myratana' (ll. 19-20, p. 1).

It is clear from the seventh design that the man with a crown is Heuxos. He is the only crowned figure who appears in the designs, and from the text it seems likely that when he and Tiriel's other sons 'rebeld' (l. 17) Heuxos took over Tiriel's title as 'king of the west' (l. 72). In the text he appears to be the 'eldest son of Tiriel' (l. 12) and to be the leader of the sons; in the designs he seems to be more passive and subservient. Heuxos reappears in the seventh and eighth designs, and perhaps in the ninth as well.

In this and the seventh design Heuxos has two companions whom the text (l. 6) identifies as brothers. In this first design the man next to King Heuxos has smooth, straight hair parted in the middle, surmounted by bay leaves, and he wears a high-waisted skirt. He reappears as the second man from the king in the seventh design, though there shorn of his bay leaves, and in the eighth design he is probably either the man shown in profile to the right of the king, or perhaps the nude man second from the king on the left. The bay leaves could indicate either a poet or a conqueror, but in the context poet seems far more likely. Unfortunately, there is nothing in the text to indicate that any of Tiriel's sons were poets.

The third man who is seen in the first drawing seems to have vine leaves in his curly hair; tendrils appear on top of his head, and by his right ear there may be a vine leaf. (If they are not vine leaves, I do not know what they are.) The vine leaves, and perhaps his nudity, may suggest that he is a celebrant, though there is nothing in the text to suggest either vine leaves or celebration. He is probably the curly-headed man beside the king in the seventh design, now without the vine leaves, and wearing instead of the mantle a loose, belted gown with a low neck. He does not seem to be among the sons in the eighth design.

In the background behind Tiriel and Myratana are three severe white columns on square bases, which in turn rest on a very low wall perhaps a foot high, and behind the sons one or more similar columns are vaguely indicated. It is not quite clear

PLATE I. Tiriel Supporting Myratana (Drawing no. I)

PLATE II. Har and Heva Bathing (Drawing no. 2)

whether the row of columns is in a straight line (in which case the perspective by Tiriel and Myratana is somewhat defective) or whether it bends slightly away from the viewer. Behind the row of columns flat ground stretches to a wide, meandering river, on the far bank of which is a high, white pyramid. In the far background, under Tiriel's hand, there seem to be distant hills.

The pyramid, the river, and the columns are not mentioned in the text, which instead describes a 'beautiful palace' (l. 1) with a 'wide court' (l. 253), which has 'Gates' (l. 1) before which Tiriel is supposed to be standing in this particular design. Nothing much like a 'Gate' appears in this design, though the locale might fairly be described as a porch. Nor is it likely that the scene is in front of the 'house' (l. 38) of King Heuxos, for this has 'lofty towers' (l. 256), which are scarcely reconcilable with the architecture shown in this first design. If, however, we take the word 'Gates' somewhat metaphorically as meaning 'entrance', the background represented here need not contradict the text, though we could never have confidently deduced those columns, or the pyramid and river, from the text.

Drawing number 2 (Pl. II)

Har and Heva are apparently sitting naked in a shallow stream with their foreheads pressed together.[1] Har's silvery beard flows to his waist, while Heva's flesh is firm and youthful. Behind them Mnetha lies on the bank in a loose, ankle-length gown, belted at the waist and secured over her left shoulder, leaving her right breast free. She is gazing over the heads of Har and Heva into the middle distance. Blake's perspective became badly distorted when he came to Mnetha's legs, which are far too long even for Blake's elongated figures. In the background are vague vertical shapes which may stand for trees and a tent. No such scene as this is described or even clearly alluded to in the text, but it may be related to the words 'they were as the shadow of Har . . . . Playing with flowers & running after birds they spent the day' (ll. 59–60, p. 3).

---

[1] In the British Museum Print Room are two drawings of about the time of *Tiriel*, one representing a black-bearded man embracing a dark-haired woman (in a position very like this second *Tiriel* drawing, though reversed) as they kneel on a rug and bolster before a figured curtain; the other represents the same couple kneeling as they warm their hands before a fire in the forest. In details of appearance and situation they bear no other close resemblance to the characters or actions of *Tiriel*.

Drawing number 3

This drawing has not been traced, so we must depend upon Rossetti's description of it:

An Ancient Man blessing or advising a Damsel, an elderly Woman by his side: all three kneeling on a bed.

A fine, careful drawing, very individual. The damsel, whose back is turned, is robed in a richly-patterned dress, unusual with Blake.

No scene very like this one is described in the poem, but it may represent the occasion when Tiriel first came to the Valley of Har, and 'Har said ["]O my mother Mnetha venture not so near him["]. . . . Mnetha said ["]Come Har & Heva rise["]' (ll. 75, 84, pp. 3, 4). Here Har is entreating Mnetha, and, as the last words indicate, Har and Heva were kneeling. The fourth design fairly clearly identifies the woman in the 'richly-patterned dress' as Mnetha.

The odd thing is that 'all three [*are*] kneeling on a bed'. Though a bed also appears in the eleventh design, no bed is described in the text. Further, before Tiriel appeared, 'Har & Heva like two children sat beneath the Oak' (l. 57), but when 'The aged father & mother saw him as they sat at play They ran weeping like frighted infants for refuge in Mnethas arms' (ll. 63-64). It is possible, though somewhat improbable, that all three should have run back to the bed before facing Tiriel. It is particularly surprising to find their protectress, Mnetha, fully dressed, on the bed. Were it not for the bed, the design, as described by Rossetti, would present no particular difficulty.

Drawing number 4 (Pl. III)

Tiriel kneels at the left in front of Har, who bends slightly forward with his hand on Tiriel's bald head, while to the right Heva grasps Mnetha fearfully around the waist and rests her head on Mnetha's breasts; Mnetha puts her right arm protectively round Heva and is apparently patting Heva's shoulder comfortingly with her left hand. The scene is quite clearly described in the text: '[*Tiriel*] kneeled down[;] . . . Har arose & laid his hand upon old Tiriels head' (ll. 84, 86, p. 4). Heva is still clinging 'for refuge in Mnethas arms' (l. 64).

Har and Tiriel have almost identical ground- and wrist-length loose gowns, though Har's is lighter than Tiriel's. Heva's gown is similar, with tucks at the waist, but she seems to have in addition a long mantle going from the back of her head to the ground. Mnetha is most strikingly dressed (as apparently she is in the third design) in a richly patterned ankle-length gown with a belt, and pleats by the calves;

PLATE III. Har Blessing Tiriel (Drawing no. 4)

PLATE IV. Tiriel Leaving Har and Heva (Drawing no. 6)

the pattern on the gown seems to represent long tendrils of foliage. On her feet are dark, shiny slippers (the only footwear seen in these designs), and her hair is caught up tightly in a checkered net or cloth. In manner and dress, particularly the striking head-covering, she is very like the nurses and some of the mothers depicted in *Songs of Innocence and of Experience* (*Innocence* title-page, 'The Ecchoing Green', the second 'Cradle Song' plate, 'Nurse's Song', 'The Fly', and 'Infant Sorrow'). Her dress and maternal attitude here are in marked contrast to those she displays in Designs 2 and 11. It is also remarkable that Mnetha and Heva are shown considerably older in this picture than they are in nos. 2 and 11.

In the background to the left are young, almost branchless trees in front of distant mountains. Behind the figures is an apparently perpendicular wall divided vertically into about five panels, which may form an angle just behind Heva. According to the text, Har, Heva, and Mnetha live in 'tents' (ll. 68, 136, 345), but it is somewhat difficult to interpret that wall as a tent. At the extreme right, behind Mnetha, is a table with a cloth over it, and behind the table there seems to be a fan-backed wicker chair. These and the luxurious bed in the eleventh design seem somewhat odd furniture for a tent, though they are not inconsistent with the rather more substantial architecture suggested by the designs.

Drawing number 5

Since the fifth design has not been located, Rossetti must be our authority for its subject: 'The Ancient Man [*Har*], and an Aged Woman [*Heva*], playing Harps.' Neither harps nor any other musical instruments are mentioned in the text, and this subject must therefore form a somewhat distant allusion to the poem. Perhaps it indicates what was in Heva's mind when she told Tiriel 'we have many sports to shew thee & many songs to sing' (l. 123, p. 5). It is not likely to be related to the words 'they sat at play' (l. 63), for the context there is games rather than music: 'Playing with flowers & running after birds they spent the day' (l. 60).

Drawing number 6 (Pl. IV)

At the right Har and Heva, dressed as they were in the fourth design, stand together in a doorway and watch blind Tiriel as he gropes his way toward the forest with the aid of a very long, straight staff. Heva appears to be bending and clinging to Har in much the same attitude in which she clung to Mnetha in the fourth drawing, while Har's arms are spread protectively round her. The scene is fairly clearly described in the text (ll. 149-52, pp. 7-8):

> Mnetha trembling at his frowns led him to the tent door
> And gave to him his staff & blest him. *He* went on his way
> But Har & Heva stood & watchd him till he enterd the wood
> And then they went & wept to Mnetha.

Behind Tiriel and on either side of the doorway are slim, young, birch-like trees, and in the distance may be seen mountains. The very solid building to the right can be seen through the doorway to have thick walls.

Drawing number 7 (Pl. V)

At the left Tiriel, on Ijim's shoulders, is apparently cursing three sons and three daughters. It is interesting to note that, though Tiriel addresses his sons here in the same way as he did at the beginning of the poem ('Come forth sons of the Curse', ll. 10, 219), in the illustration to the first scene he raises his right hand, and here he raises his left. Apparently the hand he uses when cursing is not symbolically significant; or perhaps we should note that the right-hand curse has no evident effect, while the left-hand curse is devastating.

The drawing illustrates quite clearly the passage 'Ijim raisd him up & bore him on his shoulders . . . . They [*Tiriel's sons*] stood confounde*d*, and Thus Tiriel raisd his silver voice . . . . [*Heuxos*] kneeld upon his knee' (ll. 192, 215, 233, pp. 8, 9). Though Tiriel had 'cast away my staff' earlier (l. 82), Mnetha 'gave to him his staff' when he left the tents of Har (l. 150), and he evidently carried it still while Ijim bore him on his shoulders, for it is shown in this design at Ijim's feet. Now, however, it is an ordinary curved walking-stick rather than the long straight staff shown in the sixth design.

Ijim is represented as a naked, powerful man with a magnificent curling black beard. His physique and his fierce stare accord well with the description in the text of his 'terrible strength' (l. 221) and wild habits, and help to account for the abject fear on the faces of Tiriel's children. This is apparently the only design in which Ijim is seen.

The kneeling figure is fairly clearly Heuxos, for in a deleted passage Ijim asks 'Heuxos why art thou Silent[?]' and an unidentified man replied and 'kneeld upon his knee' (ll. 226, 233). This is the same person, with a spiked crown, a pale mantle, long flowing fair hair, and a dark gown, who is also seen in the first and eighth designs. (The only differences are that in this drawing the robe seems to reach to his ankles

PLATE V. Tiriel Carried by Ijim (Drawing no. 7)

PLATE VI. Tiriel Denouncing his Four Sons and Five Daughters (Drawing no. 8)

instead of just to his knees, and he has a pale belt just below his chest. The identity of this kneeling figure and the bearded kings in the first and eighth designs makes it certain that Rossetti is mistaken when he describes 'a kneeling Queen'.)

Beside Heuxos two other men also kneel. They seem to be the same ones who are shown next to the king, but in reverse order, in the first design. If they are the same, it is significant that here they are shown without their garlands of bay and vine leaves. In a deleted passage of the text, 'Ijim said ["]Lotho Clithyma Makuth fetch your father["]' (l. 225); perhaps these kneeling men are two of the three sons whom Ijim names.

Behind the kneeling men three of Tiriel's daughters clutch each other in horror. They wear long, loose gowns, perhaps belted at the waist, very like those of Myratana, Mnetha (in the second design), and Heva. The two women at the left are conspicuously fair-haired, while the one at the right is dark. Since in the eighth drawing, where all five daughters are shown, only one has black hair, and since Hela's hair is black in the tenth and twelfth drawings, it is likely that the dark-haired woman on the right of this drawing is Hela. The text does not mention the presence of Tiriel's daughters in this scene, but it is natural that they should be there.

The background apparently represents the wall of 'Tiriels palace' (l. 194), perhaps 'the gates' themselves where Ijim entered (ll. 193-4). The wall itself is smooth and perpendicular, with a curious kind of column projecting in the centre. At the left Ijim rests on a step, and at the right, behind the daughters, the wall seems to turn a corner. In short, the background is a rectilinear building which is indicated rather than detailed.

Drawing number 8 (Pl. VI)

Amid a garland of five weeping and gesticulating kneeling daughters Tiriel stands with both arms outstretched towards the king and three other men at the right. The scene is that in which Tiriel has just pronounced his 'fathers curse . . . . The cry was great in Tiriels palace[;] his five daughters ran And caught him by the garments weeping with cries of bitter woe' (ll. 257, 260-1, p. 10). This time both Tiriel's hands are extended; clearly he is an ambidextrous curser, a right-and-left-hand swearer.

The weeping women represent all Tiriel's daughters. Four of them raise their arms to him, and three look up at him imploringly, evidently begging him to withdraw his curse. All five are dressed very much as they were in the previous drawing, and the four with raised hands are fair-haired. The only daughter with bowed head and dark hair must be Hela, who is shown with dark hair in the tenth and twelfth designs, and who was seen at the right in the seventh drawing. It is striking that she alone of the daughters seems to be already despairing. The only difficulty with this identification is that Hela in the seventh, tenth and twelfth designs, like all the other daughters for whom this detail can be observed, has bare arms, whereas the despairing daughter in this eighth design has long sleeves. This discrepancy seems to be merely an error on Blake's part, a product of the same carelessness which permitted him to lengthen the knee-length robe of the king (in nos. 1 and 8) to his ankles in the seventh design.

As usual Heuxos, the crowned king, stands in front of his brethren. He is dressed just as he was in the first design, except that he has drawn his mantle about him. The figures behind him are somewhat vaguely drawn. To the right we see a face in profile with straight, fair hair, which may be that of the bay-crowned man shown next the king in the first design, and also seen uncrowned second from the king in the seventh design. This poet could, however, also be the naked man with straight hair parted in the middle who is second to the left of the king here. The right hand of the man at the left was originally held to his head in horror, as can be seen in the unerased lines, but his arm is now shown somewhat ineffectively in front of his body. Between this man and the king can be seen a man with a black curling beard who looks much like Ijim. The text makes this identification impossible, however, for before 'Tiriels . . . five daughters ran And caught him by the garments' (ll. 260-1) 'Ijim gloomy turnd his back & silent sought The secret forests & all night wanderd in desolate ways' (ll. 241-2). This bearded man, therefore, must be one of Tiriel's sons who has not been seen before. Perhaps Heuxos' three brothers shown here are 'Lotho Clithyma Makuth' whom Ijim had addressed (l. 225). It is interesting that only two of Heuxos' brothers had been shown together before, and that one of those previously seen, the one with curly hair and vine leaves, is not shown here.

The background seems to be another section of the somewhat indeterminate stone wall of Tiriel's palace seen in the seventh design.

Drawing number 9

The untraced ninth drawing represents, according to Rossetti in 1863:

Figures kneeling near some richly-sculptured columns, seemingly in awe at some impending catastrophe.

Not quite finished, nor so remarkable as the preceding three [nos. 3, 4, 11]; yet Blake-like and mysterious.

PLATE VII. *Tiriel Walking with Hela* (Drawing no. 10)

In 1880 Rossetti reduced the title enigmatically to 'The Death of Tiriel's Sons'. They are probably appalled or stricken by Tiriel's curse:

> . . . Lo an hundred men in ghastly death[.]
> The four daughters . . .
> falln by the pestilence[;] the rest moped round in guilty fears . . . .
> Thirty of Tiriels sons remaind, to wither in the palace
> Desolate, Loathed, Dumb Astonishd waiting for black death[.]
>
> (ll. 271–7, p. 10)

Since Rossetti regularly identifies Tiriel ('The Blind Man'), Har and Heva ('The Ancient Man, and an aged Woman'), and Heuxos ('the King'), it is probable that their omission from his description of this drawing indicates that they are not present. The 'Figures' almost certainly represent Tiriel's sons.

The most remarkable part of this rather vague description is the 'richly-sculptured columns'. Nothing remotely like these has appeared in the drawings before. The architecture of Tiriel's palace, as seen in the first, seventh, and eighth designs, is rigidly rectilinear, and the only columns we have seen (in no. 1) are smooth cylinders. These 'richly-sculptured columns', then, form a powerful contrast to what we have seen of Tiriel's palace.

The only buildings mentioned in the text, besides Tiriel's palace, the caves of Zazel, and the tents and cage of Har, are the 'houses' (l. 38) and 'lofty towers' (l. 256) of Tiriel's sons, and since 'richly-sculptured columns' seem improbable in Tiriel's palace and impossible in caves, cages, or tents, it seems likely that they belong to the houses of Tiriel's sons. This would follow as well from the textual description of the scene which seems to be represented, for the curse was called down specifically upon the 'lofty towers' of the sons.

These 'lofty towers' would suggest Gothic architecture, as would the 'richly-sculptured columns'. Certainly this lavish, apparently representational decoration, whether Hindu, Greek, or Gothic, must be extraordinarily different from the severe and abstract design of Tiriel's palace shown elsewhere. Perhaps even at this time Blake believed that 'Grecian is Mathematic Form: Gothic is Living Form, Mathematic Form is Eternal in the Reasoning Memory[;] Living Form is Eternal Existence.'[1]

[1] 'On Homers Poetry [and] On Virgil.'

Drawing number 10 (Pl. VII)

Hela, with four snakes rising from her dark hair, walks across a plain with blind Tiriel, who grasps her firmly by the right arm. Her right breast is bare, as Mnetha's is in the second and eleventh designs, and a brooch secures her loose gown where it parts over her left knee. The scene comes in the text after Tiriel has cursed Hela: 'her dark hair upright stood while snakes infolded round Her madding brows . . . . She howling led him over mountains & thro frighted vales' (ll. 321-2, 327, pp. 12, 13).

In the background are 'the mountains of Har' (l. 345); they are walking east (see l. 183) through 'the valley of Har' (l. 68). The shortness of their shadows may indicate that it is 'Noon' (l. 345) when Hela's cries were first heard in the tents of Har and Heva. To right and left are trees, perhaps representing 'the wood' 'where wild beasts resort' into which 'The howling maiden led her father . . . Hoping to end her life' (ll. 341-4).

Drawing number 11 (Pl. VIII)

Har lies beneath a bedspread richly patterned with flowers, with his head beside that of Heva on an enormous bolster, while, behind Har, Mnetha watches over them protectively. The scene is probably the one just after that of the tenth drawing: 'Har & Heva slept fearless as babes on loving breasts[.] Mnetha awoke' (ll. 347-8, p. 13), though it must be confessed that line 61, 'like infants slept delighted with infant dreams', would do almost equally well. Har, Heva, and Mnetha are depicted almost exactly as they were in the second design, except that Har now has on a sleeveless, and Heva a round-necked, nightgown. Mnetha is in the same filmy gown which exposes her right breast, but her belt is no longer black. The sheeted mattress is clearly distinguishable from the bedstead, though by a mistake in perspective Blake has tucked the exotic bedspread partly under the mattress, at the foot, and partly under the bed frame. At the head of the bed there seems to be an unfigured bed-curtain, and behind this, at the left, there appears to be a rather vaguely expressed tapestry, with foliage and, in the centre, a flying Cupid.

Drawing number 12 (Pl. IX)

Tiriel lies rigidly outstretched at the edge of a clump of young trees, and at his head Hela stands with her hands in her hair as if in horror. The scene is clearly the death of Tiriel, but the text says 'He ceast outstretchd at Har & Hevas feet in awful death' (l. 393, p. 15). The woman, however, must be Hela, for she has dark hair, as

PLATE VIII. Har and Heva Asleep (Drawing no. 11)

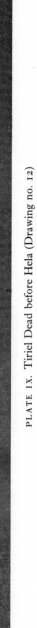

PLATE IX. Tiriel Dead before Hela (Drawing no. 12)

in the tenth design, while Heva and Mnetha (in nos. 2, 4, 11) and the other four daughters (nos. 7, 8) are fair-haired. Further, she has on the same dark-belted loose gown parting over the left knee that we saw on Hela in the tenth design, though now the brooch is gone. We need not be concerned that she no longer has snakes in her hair as she did in the tenth drawing, for Tiriel had promised her that the 'curse of Tiriel Shall fail' after Hela led him to Har and Heva (ll. 325-6). We can be fairly confident, then, that the woman represented is Hela.

The difficulty is that the text specifies that Tiriel was 'outstretchd at Har & Hevas feet', and Har and Heva are nowhere to be seen. However, it is natural to expect Hela to be still present as she was at the beginning of Tiriel's speech (l. 355), and her horror at the death of her father is also natural. Apparently this design is one more indication of the ways in which Blake emended or made more specific the implications of the text.

Just beyond Tiriel's body are rows of thickly set young trees, with grape vines in heavy fruit twining round them. Probably this is 'the lower garden' at which Mnetha had met Tiriel and Hela (l. 351).

History of the Manuscript

Nothing is certainly known of the *Tiriel* manuscript and drawings before 1863. In that year, on 1 May, the twelve drawings were sold at Christie's (see History of the Drawings, p. 27). In his catalogue, published in Gilchrist's *Life*, W. M. Rossetti could not say confidently what the drawings illustrated, but in 1868 Swinburne was sure that the text of *Tiriel* and the twelve designs belonged together,[1] and he in turn persuaded W. M. Rossetti.[2] Rossetti had read the poem by 1863, and in 1874 he wrote that the 'MS. was, until recently, the property of Mrs. Gilchrist'.[3] Swinburne quoted from the poem in 1868, though he found it 'weak and inadequate',[1] and the whole poem was published, in a somewhat tidier form than Blake left it in, by W. M. Rossetti in 1874.[4] A fresh but not remarkably accurate transcript was made by W. B. Yeats and E. J. Ellis in 1893.[5] A new, accurate transcript was published

[1] Algernon Charles Swinburne, *William Blake* (London, 1868), p. 199 fn.

[2] *The Poetical Works of William Blake*, ed. W. M. Rossetti (London, 1874), p. cxxiii; Alexander Gilchrist, *Life of William Blake* (London and Cambridge, 1880), vol. ii, p. 273.

[3] *The Poetical Works of William Blake*, ed. W. M. Rossetti (London, 1874), p. cxxiii.

[4] Ibid., pp. 207-31.

[5] *The Works of William Blake*, eds. W. B. Yeats and E. J. Ellis (London, 1893), vol. iii, pp. 3-16; *The Poems of William Blake*, ed. W. B. Yeats (London, 1893), pp. 147-61; *The Poetical Works of William Blake*, ed. Edwin J. Ellis (London, 1906), vol. i, pp. 271-91.

by John Sampson with bibliographical notes in 1913,[1] and other responsible trans-
cripts were published by Geoffrey Keynes in 1925,[2] by Sloss and Wallis in 1926,[3]
by Robert Gleckner in 1959,[4] and by D. V. Erdman in 1965.[5] All the twentieth-
century texts here offer responsible readings, and the differences consist mainly in
the confidence with which difficult words are read. The chief exception is with
Gleckner's and Erdman's texts, which for the first time present the punctuation as
Blake left it. The text given below differs essentially from Gleckner's and Erdman's,
I believe, only in a few difficult readings, mostly in deletions.

The manuscript itself was lost sight of for some time after W. M. Rossetti published it in 1874. It was found again in a box in the office of George Bell & Son,
Rossetti's publisher,[6] and sold as Lot 458 in the Sotheby sale of 29 July 1903. There
it was bought by Quaritch, and, as the inscription now on the manuscript states, it
was 'Purchased of B. Quaritch, 13 Feb. 1909' from the Farnborough Fund of the
British Museum, and it is now catalogued in the British Museum Department of
Manuscripts as Egerton 2876.

The uniform consensus of scholarly opinion is that *Tiriel* was composed early in
Blake's mature literary career,[7] but the justification for this consensus is not over-
whelming. The handwriting seems to be fairly early, but this evidence cannot be
very precise, for we have no handwriting by Blake which can be conclusively dated
much before 1790. The style of the drawings is somewhat stiff and constrained,
compared with Blake's later work, and is similar to that in other designs he made
about 1790, but this too is rather vague evidence, even if we presume that the text

---

[1] *The Poetical Works of William Blake*, ed.
John Sampson (London, 1913).

[2] *The Writings of William Blake*, ed. Geoffrey
L. Keynes (London, 1925), vol. i, pp. 133–48;
Keynes somewhat normalized the text which he
frequently printed in *Poetry and Prose of William
Blake* (1927–61). The statement in his edition of
The Complete Writings of William Blake (London
and New York, 1957), p. 886, that 'The present text
[*pp. 99–110, was*] . . . collated with the original
MS' appears to refer to 1925 rather than to 1957.

[3] *The Prophetic Writings of William Blake*,
eds. D. J. Sloss and J. P. R. Wallis (London,
1926), vol. ii, pp. 278–89.

[4] Robert Gleckner, *The Piper & the Bard*
(Detroit, 1959), pp. 131–42.

[5] *The Poetry and Prose of William Blake*, ed.
D. V. Erdman, commentary by Harold Bloom
(New York, 1965), pp. 273–82, 735–6.

[6] Edwin J. Ellis, *The Real Blake* (London,
1906), pp. 158–9.

[7] *The Poetical Works of William Blake*, ed.
W. M. Rossetti (London, 1874), p. cxxiii; *The
Poems of William Blake*, ed. W. B. Yeats (Lon-
don, 1893), p. 249; *The Poetical Works of
William Blake*, ed. John Sampson (Oxford, 1905),
p. 330; Geoffrey Keynes, *A Bibliography of
William Blake* (New York, 1921); *The Complete
Writings of William Blake*, ed. G. Keynes (Lon-
don and New York, 1957), p. 886; S. Foster
Damon, *William Blake His Philosophy and
Symbols* (Boston, 1924), p. 71; *The Prophetic
Writings of William Blake*, eds. D. J. Sloss and
J. P. R. Wallis (Oxford, 1926), vol. ii, p. 275;
D. V. Erdman, *Blake Prophet against Empire*
(Princeton, 1954), pp. 120–2; Robert Gleck-
ner, *The Piper & the Bard* (Detroit, 1959),
p. 143.

and designs must have been made at the same time. The facts that the poem is incomplete, with some lines left unfinished, and that the narrative and the characters scarcely reappear in Blake's later myth suggest that he was experimenting with the vehicle for his cosmological ideas, and that therefore *Tiriel* must precede most of his Prophecies. The fact that Blake never engraved *Tiriel*, though it is shorter than some of the works in Illuminated Printing of the 1790's, may imply that he had not yet fully developed his own printing technique. Similarly, the absence of designs on the pages of text, and the difference in shape and style between the separate *Tiriel* designs and those for all Blake's other Illuminated Works, suggest that he was not preparing to publish *Tiriel* himself, and that he had not yet proved to himself the feasibility of publishing such a work by his own method of printing. Since by 1789 Blake was energetically publishing his own writings, with *Thel* and *Songs of Innocence*, it seems safe from this evidence to date *Tiriel* no later than about 1789. Some confirmation of the inference that *Tiriel* precedes *Thel* (1789) and the other works in Illuminated Printing may be found in the fact that one deleted line of *Tiriel* (l. 370) appears unchanged in Thel's Motto. Whether or not Blake deleted the line in *Tiriel* because he was going to use it in *Thel*, it does seem to imply priority in *Tiriel*. Similarly, line 360 reappears scarcely changed in the *Marriage of Heaven and Hell* (1790?) and this would also suggest that *Tiriel* precedes the *Marriage*.

Finally, the symbolism and thematic concern of *Tiriel* seem to show Blake working out the relationship between helpless innocence in Har and Heva and self-destroying experience in Tiriel,[1] and it is reasonable to date Blake's concern with this theme between about 1784 (the date of the first drafts of *Innocence* in the *Island in the Moon*) and 1789, when Blake was turning to themes and songs of *Experience*. All these rather nebulous indications seem to point to a date when Blake was bringing to earliest fruition his techniques of Prophecy, Illumination, and Printing. The agreed-upon date of 1789 seems satisfactory enough if we recognize that none of our evidence would very convincingly contradict a date as much as, perhaps, four years on either side of this one.

Description of the Manuscript

The manuscript consists of eight leaves enclosed within light blue-grey paper wrappers, which are bound in blue morocco, with a stamped coat of arms on the inside of the front cover and again on the blank verso of the last leaf, indicating that

---

[1] Robert Gleckner, *The Piper & the Bard* (Detroit, 1959), pp. 142-56.

it was bought from the Farnborough Fund left by the Earl of Bridgewater to the British Museum. Page 6 has the Egerton stamp on it. The front wrapper is inscribed in old ink in a hand which has been ascribed to Blake: 'Tiriel / MS by M ͬ Blake'.

The pages are 15·7 cm. wide by 21·0 cm. high (slightly smaller than the drawings, which are about 27× 18 cm.) and are mounted together with the blue wrappers on stubs. All the leaves have an undated watermark of the Britannia type, with the countermark G R (see Plate X).[1] There is no lettering in the rim of the watermarked circle. No leaf shows the whole watermark.

In each leaf and in the blue wrappers there are two sets of three stab holes (six holes in all) very near to each other, perhaps indicating that the manuscript was stabbed for sewing three times. The top group is 5·0 cm. from the top of the leaf, and the second group is 5·0 cm. from the first, though these distances are somewhat approximate, for the relationships vary slightly. It is important to note that these sets of stab holes appear in the left margins of the rectos throughout. The last two leaves (pp. 13–16) differ from the others in having a set of five stab holes in the bottom margin as well. Naturally no thread remains in any of these stab holes.

The rectos of the leaves are foliated 1–7 in ink, in the top centre of the page, on pages 1, 3, 5, 7, *10* [*N.B.*], 11, and 13. The last page, 15, needed no number, for it is obviously the last page of the poem: the text stops a quarter of the way down the page with the words 'He ceast outstretchd at Har & Hevas feet in awful death'.

It is harder to explain the misnumbering on page 10, which is a verso instead of a recto like the other numbered pages. The '5' on page 10 implies that the order of the pages should be 1–8, 10, 9, 11–15, but the continuity of the narrative clearly demonstrates that the present order is the correct one. At the end of page 8, after Ijim has brought in Tiriel and said 'fetch your father fetch forth Myratana', Tiriel echoes him ironically: 'Serpents not sons why do you stand[?] fetch hither Tiriel' (ll. 214, 216). Page 9 follows very naturally with 'Fetch hither Myratana', but page 10 begins 'And aged Tiriel stood & said ["]where does the thunder sleep[?"]' (l. 243). This clear narrative continuity is confirmed by the stab holes, which demonstrate unmistakably that, whatever the *order* of the leaves, the present rectos were also rectos when the leaves were first stabbed.

The rectos are also correctly foliated in pencil 2–9 on the top right corner of pages 1, 3, 5, 7, 9, 11, 13, and 15. Probably neither foliation is Blake's.

---

[1] The main watermark is a triple circle surmounted by a bulbous crown. Within the circle stands Britannia by her shield, which has a cross on it, and she holds a spear. The type is common in Edward Heawood, *Watermarks* (Hilversum, 1950) and in W. A. Churchill, *Watermarks in Paper* (Amsterdam, 1935); it is not identical with any watermark reproduced there, though it is most like Churchill nos. 220, 221, 233.

a. Britannia Watermark in *Tiriel*

b. Crowned G R Countermark in *Tiriel*

PLATE X

The same grey-black ink is used throughout the poem, with very minor changes. Ultraviolet light brings up no more from the manuscript than may be seen by the naked eye. Blake has used a clear but not a copperplate hand, and though there are numerous changes in the text, including some thirty-nine deleted lines, there are few enough minor alterations to make one wonder on this evidence whether this was intended as a fair copy.

Curiosity as to whether this is a fair copy is intensified by the strange way in which the pages are filled with writing. Three-fifths of the pages are full from top to bottom (pp. 1, 3–5, 7–8, 10–11, 14), averaging thirty-two lines to the page (twenty-seven to thirty-six lines). The other pages are left partly blank at the bottom, in mid narrative, for no clear reason. These blank spaces range from three-quarters of the page on the last page (p. 15), as is natural, through half the page on pages 6 and 12 to a tenth of the page on page 9, and the average number of lines on these pages (pp. 2, 6, 9, 12, 13, 15) is seventeen. These partially blank pages do not seem to be related to where the drawings come, for only one or two of the blank spaces occur near where one would expect a design to be. That is, there seems to be no evidence that Blake was spacing the writing as he would have to when it was engraved, leaving blank spaces for the designs to come in. I can suggest no likely explanation of why some of the pages should be so incompletely filled.

Symbols Used in the Transcript

With such a brief manuscript, very few symbols are needed, and most of those used are conventional.

[145]   The line numbers in square brackets count both deleted and standing lines.

[aged *del*] Deleted words are given within square brackets; editorial interpolations within square brackets such as '*del*' for '*deleted*' are given in italics.

[*Page 1*]   Page numbers are inserted thus within square brackets. (The page numbers that actually appear in the manuscript are omitted in the transcript because they are inconsistent and confusing, but they may be reconstructed from the 'Description of the Manuscript'.)

Because the manuscript is a draft with Blake's characteristically anarchic punctuation, some special symbols are needed. I have tried to give the text of the poem as exactly as type can reproduce handwriting, with five exceptions:

1. Blake's long 's' is consistently normalized.
2. Sometimes Blake started to write a word and deleted it before he had completed more than one or two letters, which are now illegible, as in line 19: 'the aged man [h(?) *del*] raisd up his right hand'. I have ignored these slips when they are not clearly legible. They occur in lines 19, 33, 35, 87, 88, 106, 148, 219, 333.
3. Where Blake has put in a meaningless period, I have omitted the period, but the omission is indicated by the italic terminal letter of the word which preceded the period. When the period seems to do duty for another mark of punctuation, I have substituted the mark Blake apparently intended. For example, in lines 5–6 Blake wrote 'the Voice Of aged Tiriel. arose. that his sons might hear', but the transcript here reads 'the Voice Of aged Tirie*l* arose, that his sons might hear'. Each punctuation mark following these terminal italic letters is an editorial substitution for the period Blake left there.
4. I have not indicated where Blake altered the original lower case letter to a capital.
5. Sometimes Blake put a period in the middle of a line in what seems to be a reasonable place, but the word succeeding the period begins with a lower case

letter. I have arbitrarily capitalized these initial letters as they seemed to call for it, but to indicate the editorial alteration the capital letter is italicized. Thus in line 109, 'I remain an outcast. *H*ast thou any thing to drink', the italic capital *H* was left lower case by Blake.

I hope that these symbols will prove unobtrusive but traceable when necessary.

TRANSCRIPT AND
FACSIMILE OF *TIRIEL*

[Page 1]

And Aged Tirie*l* stood before the Gates of his beautiful palace
[But dark were his once piercing eyes *del*]
With Myratan*a*, once the Queen of all the western plains[,]
But now his eyes were darkne*d*, & his wife fading in death[.]
[5] They stood before their once delightful palac*e*, & thus the Voice
Of aged Tirie*l* aros*e*, that his sons might hear in their gates[:]

["]Accursed race of T*i*rie*l*, behold your [aged *del*] father[.]
Come forth & look on her that bore you. *C*ome you accursed sons.
In my weak [aged *del*] arm*s* I here have borne your dying mother[.]
[10] Come forth sons of the Curse come forth see the death of Myratana[."]

The sons ran from their gate*s* & saw their aged parents stand
And thus the eldest son of Tiriel raisd his might*y* voice[:]

["]Old man unworthy to be call*d* the father of Tiriels race[,]
For every one of those thy wrinkle*s*, each of those grey hairs
[15] Are cruel as deat*h* & as obdurate as the devouring pit[.]
Why should thy sons care for thy curses thou accursed man[?]
Were we not slaves till we rebel*d*? Who cares for Tiriels curse[?]
His blessing was a cruel curse. His curse may be a blessing[."]

He ceast[;] the aged man raisd up his right hand to the heavens[;]
[20] His left supported Myratana [Living(?) *del*] shrinking in pangs of death[.]
The orbs of his large eyes he open*d*, & thus his voice went forth[:]

["]Serpents not son*s*, wreathing around the bones of Tiriel[,]
Ye worms of death feasting upon your aged parents flesh[,]
Listen & hear your mothers groans. No more accursed Sons
[25] She bears. *S*he groans not at the birth of Heuxos or Yuva[.]
These are the groans of death[,] ye serpents[,] These are the groans of death[.]
Nourishd with milk ye serpent*s*, nourishd with mothers tears & cares[.]
Look at my eyes blind as the orbless scull among the stones[,]
Look at my bald head. Hark listen ye serpents [all(?) *del*] listen[!]
[30] What Myratana. What my wife O Soul O Spirit O fire[!]
What Myratana. *A*rt thou dea*d*? Look here ye serpents look[!]
The serpents sprung from her own bowels have draind her dry as this[.]

1

And aged Tiriel. stood before the gates of his beautiful palace

~~Est ~~ ~~ ~~ ~~ ~~ ~~ ~~ ~~ ~~ ~~ ~~~~

With Myratana. once the Queen of all the western plains
But now his eyes were darkned. & his wife fading in death
They stood before their once delightful palace. & thus the Voice
Of aged Tiriel. arose. that his sons might hear in their gates

Accursed race of Tiriel. behold your ~~aged~~ father
Come forth & look on her that bore you. come you accursed sons.
In my weak ~~aged~~ arms. I here have borne your dying mother
Come forth sons of the Curse come forth. see the death of Myratana.

His sons ran from their gates. & saw their aged parents stand
And thus the eldest son of Tiriel raisd his mighty voice

Old man unworthy to be calld. the father of Tiriels race
For every one of those thy wrinkles. each of those grey hairs
Are cruel as death. & as obdurate as the devouring pit
Why should thy sons care for thy curses thou accursed man
Were we not slaves till we rebeld. Who cares for Tiriels curse
His blessing was a cruel curse. His curse may be a blessing

He ceast the ~~aged~~ man & raisd up his right hand to the heavens
His left supported Myratana ~~shrinking~~ in pangs of death
The orbs of his large eyes he opend. & thus his voice went forth

Serpents not sons. wreathing around the bones of Tiriel
Ye worms of death feasting upon your aged parents flesh
Listen & hear your mothers groans. No more accursd Sons
She bears. she groans not at the birth of Heuxos or Yuva
These are the groans of death ye serpents These are the groans of death
Nourishd with milk ye serpents. nourishd with mothers tears & care
Look at my eyes blind as the orbless scull among the stones
Look at my bald head. Hark listen ye serpents ~~listen~~ listen
What Myratana. What my wife O Soul O Spirit O fire
What Myratana. art thou dead. Look here ye serpents look
The serpents sprung from her own bowels have drained her dry as this

PLATE XI

[Page 2]

Curse on your ruthless head*s*, for I will bury her even here[."]

So saying he began to dig a grave with his aged hands
[35] But Heuxos calld a son of Zaze*l* to dig their mother a grave[.]

["]Old cruelty[,] desist & let us dig a grave for thee[.]
Thou hast refusd our charity[,] thou hast refusd our food[,]
Thou hast refusd our clothes our beds our houses for thy dwelling
Chusing to wander like a Son of Zazel in the rocks[.]
[40] Why dost thou curs*e*; is not the curse now come upon your head[?]
Was it not you enslavd the sons of Zaze*l*, & they have cursd
And now you feel it. Dig a grave & let us bury our mother[."]

["]There take the bod*y*, cursed son*s*, & may the heavens rain wrath
As thick as northern fog*s* around your gate*s* to choke you up
[45] That you may lie as now your mother lie*s*, like dog*s* cast out[,]
The stin*k* of your dead carcase*s* annoying man & beast
Till your white bones are bleachd with age for a memorial[.]
No your remembrance shall peris*h*, for when your carcases
Lie stinking on the eart*h*, the buriers shall arise from the east
[50] An*d* not a bone of all the sons of Tiriel remain[.]
Bury your mother but you cannot bury the curse of Tiriel[."]

He ceast & darkling oer the mountains sought his pathless way[.]

Curse on your ruthless heads. for I will bury her even here

So saying he began to dig a grave with his aged hands
But Heuxos calld a son of Zazel. to dig their mother a grave

Old cruelty desist & let us dig a grave for thee
Thou hast refusd our charity thou hast refusd our food
Thou hast refusd our clothes our beds our houses for thy dwelling
Chusing to wander like a Son of Zazel in the rocks
Why dost thou curse. is not the curse now come upon your head
Was it not you enslavd the sons of Zazel & they have cursd
And now you feel it. Dig a grave & let us bury our mother

There take the body. cursd sons. & may the heavens rain wrath
As thick as northern fogs. around your gates. to choke you up
That you may lie as now your mother lies. like dogs. cast out
The stink. of your dead carcases. annoying man & beast
Till your white bones are bleachd with age for a memorial.
No your remembrance shall perish. for when your carcases
Lie stinking on the earth. the briaries shall arise from the east
And. not a bone of all the sons of Tiriel remain
Bury your mother but you cannot bury the curse of Tiriel

He ceast & darkling oer the mountains sought his pathless way

PLATE XII

He wanderd day & night[;] to him both day & night were dark[.]
The sun he felt but the bright moon was now a useless globe[.]
[55] Oer mountains & thro vales of wo*e*, the blind & aged man
Wanderd till he that leadeth al*l* led him to the vales of Har

And Har & Heva like two children sat beneath the Oak[.]
Mnetha now aged waited on the*m*, & brought them food & clothing
But they were as the shadow of Ha*r*, & as the years forgotten[,]
[60] Playing with flower*s* & running after birds they spent the day
And in the night like infants slept delighted with infant dreams[.]

Soon as the blind wanderer enterd the pleasant gardens of Har
[The aged father & mother saw him as they sat at play *all del*]
They ran weeping like frighted infants for refuge in Mnethas arms[.]
[65] The blind man felt his way & cried ["]*P*eace to these open doors[.]
Let no one fear[,] for poor blind Tiriel hurts none but himself[.]
Tell me O friends where I am no*w*, & in what pleasant place[."]

["]This is the valley of Har[,"] said Mnetha ["]& this the tent of Har[.]
Who art thou poor blind ma*n*, that takest the name of Tiriel on thee[?]
[70] Tiriel is king of all the west. *W*ho art thou[?] I am Mnetha
And this is Har & Hev*a*, trembling like infants by my side[."]

["]I know Tiriel is king of the west & there he lives in joy[.]
No matter who I am O Mnetha. *If* thou hast any food
Give it m*e*, for I cannot stay[;] my journey is far from hence[."]

[75] Then Har said ["]O my mother Mnetha venture not so near him
For he is the king of rotten wood & of the bones of death[.]
He wander*s* without eye*s* & passes thro thick walls & doors[.]
Thou shalt not smite my mother Mnetha O thou eyeless man[."]

[O venerable O most piteous O most woeful day *all del*]
[80] ["]A wander*er*, I beg for food. *Y*ou see I cannot weep[.]
[But I can kneel down at your door. I am a harmless man *all del*]
I cast away my staff the kind companion of my travel
And I kneel down that you may see I am a harmless man[."]

2   3

He wanderd day & night to him both day & night were dark
The sun he felt but the bright moon was now a eyeless globe
Oer mountains & thro vales of woe. the blind & aged man
Wanderd till he that leadeth all. led him to the vales of Har

And Har & Heva like two children sat beneath the Oak
Mnetha now aged waited on them. & brought them food & clothing
But they were as the shadows of Har. & as the years forgotten
Playing with flowers. & running after birds they spent the day
And in the night like infants slept delighted with infant dreams

Soon as the blind wanderer enterd the pleasant gardens of Har
~~They ran weeping like frighted infants for refuge in Mnethas arms~~
They ran weeping like frighted infants for refuge in Mnethas arms
The blind man felt his way & cried peace to these open doors
Let no one fear for poor blind Tiriel hurts none but himself
Tell me O friend where am I now. & in what pleasant place

This is the valley of Har said Mnetha & this the tent of Har
Who art thou poor blind man. that takest the name of Tiriel on thee
Tiriel is king of all the west who art thou I am Mnetha
And this is Har & Heva. trembling like infants by my side

I know Tiriel is king of the west & there he lives in joy
No matter who I am O Mnetha. if thou hast any food
Give it me. for I cannot stay my journey is far from hence

Then Har said O my mother Mnetha venture not so near him
For he is the king of rotten wood & of the bones of death
He wanders without eyes. & passes thro thick walls & doors
Thou shalt not smite my mother Mnetha O thou eyeless man

~~Venerable & very piteous O most woeful day~~
A wanderer. I beg for food. you see I cannot weep
~~But I can kneel down at your door I am a harmless man~~
I cast away my staff the kind companion of my travel
And I kneel down that you may see I am a harmless man

PLATE XIII

66

[Page 4]

He kneeled down & Mnetha said ["]Come Har & Heva rise[.]
[85] He is an innocent old man & hungry with his travel[."]

Then Har arose & laid his hand upon old Tiriels head[.]

["]God bless thy poor bald pate. God bless thy hollow winking eyes[.]
God bless thy shriveld beard. God bless thy many wrinkled forehead[.]
Thou hast no teeth old man & thus I kiss thy sleek bald head[.]
[90] Heva come kiss his bald head for he will not hurt us Heva[."]

Then Heva came & took old Tiriel in her mothers arms[.]

["]Bless thy poor eyes old ma*n*, & bless the old father of Tiriel[.]
Thou art my Tiriels old father. I know thee thro thy wrinkles
Because thou smelles*t* like the figtre*e*, thou smellest like ripe figs[.]
[95] How didst thou lose thy eyes old Tirie*l*? *B*less thy wrinkled face[."]

[The aged Tiriel could not speak his heart was full of grief
He strove against his rising passions. but still he could not speak *all del*]

Mnetha said ["]come in aged wanderer[,] tell us of thy name[.]
Why shouldest thou conceal thyself from those of thine own flesh[?"]

[100] ["]I am not of this regio*n*["] said Tiriel dissemblingly[.]
[Fearing to tell them who he was. because of the weakness of Har *all del*]
["]I am an aged wanderer once father of a race
Far in the nort*h*, but they were wicked & were all destroyd
And I their father sent an outcast. I have told you all[.]
[105] Ask me no more I pray for grief hath seald my precious sight[:"]

["]O Lord[,"] said Mnetha ["]how I tremble[;] are there then more people
More human creatures on this earth beside the sons of Har[?"]

["]No more[,"] said Tiriel ["]but I remain on all this globe
And I remain an outcast. *H*ast thou any thing to drink[?"]

[110] Then Mnetha gave him milk & fruit*s*, & they sat down together[.]

He kneeled down & Mnetha said Come Har & Heva rise
He is an innocent old man & hungry with his travel

Then Har arose & laid his hand upon old Tiriels head

God bless thy poor bald pate. God bless. thy hollow wrinkling eyes
God bless thy shrivel'd beard. God. bless. thy many wrinkled forehead
Thou hast no teeth old man & thus I kiss thy sleek bald head
Heva come kiss his bald head for he will not hurt us Heva

Then Heva came & took old Tiriel in her mothers arms

Bless thy poor eyes old man. & bless the old father of Tiriel
Thou art my Tiriels old father. I know thee thro thy wrinkles
Because thou smellest like the fig tree. thou smellest like ripe figs
How didst thou lose thy eyes old Tiriel. bless thy wrinkled face

The aged Tiriel could not speak his heart was full of grief
He strove against his rising passions. but still he could not speak
Mnetha said come in aged wanderer tell us of thy name
Why shouldest thou conceal thyself from those of thine own flesh

I am not of this region. said Tiriel dissemblingly
Fearing to tell them who he was. because of the weakness of Har
I am an aged wanderer once father of a race
Far in the north. but they were wicked & were all destroyd
And I their father sent an outcast. I have told you all
Ask me no more I pray for grief hath seald my precious sight

O Lord said Mnetha how I tremble are there then more people
More human creatures on this earth beside the sons of Har

No more said Tiriel but I remain on all this globe
And I remain an outcast. hast thou any thing to drink

Then Mnetha gave him milk & fruits. & they sat down together

PLATE XIV

They sat & eat & Har & Heva smild on Tiriel[.]

["]Thou art a very old old man but I am older than thou[.]
How came thine hair to leave thy forehead[?] *How* came thy face so brown[?]
My hair is very long[,] my bear*d* doth cover all my breast[.]
[115] God bless thy piteous face. *T*o count the wrinkles in thy face
Would puzzle [Har(*?*) *del*] Mnetha. *B*less thy face for thou art Tiriel[."]

[Tiriel could scarce dissemble more & his tongue could scarce refrain
But still he feard that Har & Heva would die of joy & grief *all del*]

["]Tiriel I never saw but once[.] I sat with him & eat[.]
[120] He was as chearful as a prince & gave me entertainment
But long I staid not at his palace for I am forcd to wander[."]

["]What wilt thou leave us too[?"] said Heva ["]thou shalt not leave us too
For we have many sports to shew thee & many songs to sing
And after dinner we will walk into the cage of Har
[125] And thou shalt help us to catch bird*s* & gather them ripe cherries[.]
Then let thy name be Tiriel & never leave us more[."]

["]If thou dost go[,"] said Har ["]I wish thine eyes may see thy folly[.]
My sons have left me[;] did thine leave thee[?] O twas very cruel[!"]

["]No venerable man[,"] said Tiriel ["]ask me not such things
[130] For thou dost make my heart to bleed[;] my sons were not like thine
But worse[.] O never ask me more or I must flee away[."]

["]Thou shalt not go[,"] said Heva ["]till thou hast seen our singing birds
And [H *del*] heard Har sing in the great cage & slept upon our fleeces[.]
Go not for thou art so like Tirie*l*, that I love thine head
[135] Tho it is wrinkled like the earth parchd with the summer heat[."]

Then Tiriel rose up from the seat & said ["]god bless these tents[.]
[God bless my benefactors for I cannot tarry longer *all del*]
My Journey is oer rocks & mountain*s*, not in pleasant vales[.]
I must not sleep nor rest because of madness & dismay[."]

[140] [Then Mnetha led him to the door & gave to him his staff *all del*]

3

They sat & eat & Har & Heva smil'd on Tiriel

4

Thou art a very old old man but I am older than thou
How came thine hairs to leave thy forehead how came thy face so brown
My hair is very long my beard doth cover all my breast
God bless thy piteous face. to count the wrinkles in thy face
Would puzzle ~~the~~ Mnetha. bless thy face for thou art Tiriel

~~Tiriel could scarce dissemble more & his tongue could scarce refrain~~
~~But still he feard that Har & Heva would die of joy & grief~~

Tiriel I never saw but once I sat with him & eat
He was as chearful as a prince & gave me entertainment
But long I staid not at his palace for I am forc'd to wander

What wilt thou leave us too said Heva thou shalt not leave us too
For we have many sports to shew thee & many songs to sing
And after dinner we will walk into the cage of Har
And thou shalt help us to catch birds & gather them ripe cherries
Then let thy name be Tiriel & never leave us more

If thou dost go said Har I wish thine eyes may see thy folly
My sons have left me did thine leave thee O twas very cruel

No venerable man said Tiriel ask me not such things
For thou dost make my heart to bleed my sons were not like these
But worse O never ask me more or I must flee away

Thou shalt not go said Heva till thou hast seen our singing birds
And heard Har sing in the great cage & slept upon our fleeces
Go not for thou art so like Tiriel that I love thine head
Tho it is wrinkled like the earth parch'd with the summer heat

Then Tiriel rose up from the seat & said god bless these tents
~~for all my journey long I cannot tarry~~
My journey is oer rocks & mountains not in pleasant vales
I must not sleep nor rest because of madness & dismay

PLATE XV

[Page 6]

[And Har & Heva stood & watchd him till he enterd the wood
[And then they went & wept to Mnetha but they soon forgot their tears *all del*]

[But *del*] And Mnetha said ["]Thou must not go to wander dar*k* alone
But dwell with us & let us be to thee instead of eyes
[145] And I will bring thee food old ma*n*, till death shall call thee hence[."]

Then Tiriel frownd & answer*d*: ["]Did I not command you saying
Madness & deep dismay possess the heart of the blind man
The wanderer who [runs *del*] seeks the woods leaning upon his staff[?"]

Then Mnetha trembling at his frowns led him to the tent door
[150] And gave to him his staff & blest him. *H*e went on his way[.]

But Har & Heva stood & watchd him till he enterd the wood
And then they went & wept to Mneth*a*, but they soon forgot their tears[.]

[Page 6]

~~[crossed out lines]~~

And Mnetha said Thou must not go to wander dark. alone
But dwell with us & let us be to thee instead of eyes
And I will bring thee food O man. till death shall call thee hence

Then Tiriel frownd & answerd. Did I not command you saying
Madness & deep dismay possess the heart of the blind man
The wanderer who seeks the woods leaning upon his staff

Then Mnetha trembling at his frowns led him to the tent door
And gave to him his staff & blest him. he went on his way

But Har & Heva stood & watchd him till he enterd the wood
And then they went & wept to Mnetha. but they soon forgot their tears

PLATE XVI

[Page 7]

Over the weary hills the blind man took his lonely way[.]
To him the day & night alike were dark & desolate
[155] But far he had not gone when Ijim from his woods come down
Met him at entrance of the forest in a dark & lonely way[.]

["]Who art thou Eyeless wretch that thus obstructst the lions path[?]
Ijim shall rend thy feeble joints thou tempter of dark Ijim[.]
Thou hast the form of Tiriel but I know thee well enough[.]
[160] Stand from my path foul fiend[;] is this the last of thy deceits
To be a hypocrite & stand in shape of a blind beggar[?"]

The blind man heard his brothers voice & kneeld down on his knee[.]

["]O brother Ijim if it is thy voice that speaks to me
Smite not thy brother Tiriel tho weary of his life[.]
[165] My sons have smitten me alread*y*, and if thou smitest me
The curse that rolls over their heads will rest itself on thine[.]
Tis now seven years since in my palace I beheld thy face[."]
[Seven years of sorrow then the curse of Zazel *all del*]

["]Come thou dark fiend I dare thy cunning[;] know that Ijim scorns
[170] To smite the[*e*] in the form of helpless age & eyeless policy[.]
Rise up for I discern thee & I dare thy eloquent tongue[.]
Come I will lead thee on thy way & use thee as a scoff[."]

["]O Brother Ijim thou beholdest wretched Tiriel[.]
Kiss me my brother & then leave me to wander desolate[."]

[175] ["]No artful fien*d*, but I will lead thee[;] dost thou want to go[?]
Reply not lest I bind thee with the green flags of the brook[.]
Ay now thou art discoverd I will use thee like a slave[."]

When Tiriel heard the words of Ijim he sought not to reply[.]
He knew twas vain for Ijims words were as the voice of Fate[.]

[180] And they went on together over hills thro woody vales
Blind to the pleasures of the sight & deaf to warbling birds[.]
All day they walkd & all the night beneath the pleasant Moon
Westwardly journeying till Tiriel grew weary with his travel[.]

["]O Ijim I am faint & weary for my knees forbid
[185] To bear me further. *U*rge me not lest I should die with travel[.]

5

Oeer the weary hills the blind man took his lonely way
To him the day & night alike was dark & desolate
But far he had not gone when Tiriel from his wood come down
Met him at entrance of the forest in a dark & lonely way

Who art thou Eyeless wretch that thus obstructs the lions path
Tiriel shall rend thy feeble joints thou tempter of dark Tiriel
Thou hast the form of Tiriel but I know thee well enough
Stand from my path foul fiend is this the last of thy deceits
To be a hypocrite & stand in shape of a blind beggar

The blind man heard his brothers voice & kneeld down on his knee

O brother Tiriel if it is thy voice that speaks to me
Smite not thy brother Tiriel tho weary of his life
My sons have smitten me already. and if thou smitest me
The curse that rolls over their heads will rest itself on thine   Tis now seven years since in my
                                                                        palace I beheld thy face
Come thou dark fiend I dare thy cunning know that Tiriel scorns   ~~thine eyes ~~ ~~~~ then
To smite thee in the form of helpless age & eyeless policy   ~~~~~~~~~
Rise up for I discern thee & I dare thy eloquent tongue
Come I will lead thee on thy way & use thee as a scoff

O Brother Tiriel thou beholdest wretched Tiriel
Kiss me my brother & then leave me to wander desolate

No artful fiend. but I will lead thee dost thou want to go
Reply not lest I bind thee with the green flags of the brook
Ay now thou art discoverd I will use thee like a slave

When Tiriel heard the words of Tiriel he sought not to reply
He knew twas vain for Tiriels word were as the voice of Fate

And they went on together over hills thro woody dales
Blind to the pleasures of the sight & deaf to warbling birds
All day they walkd & all the night beneath the pleasant Moon
Westwardly journeying till Tiriel grew weary with his travel

O Tiriel I am faint & weary for my knees forbed
To bear me further. urge me not lest I should die with travel

PLATE XVII

74

[Page 8]

A little rest I crave a little water from a brook
Or I shall soon discover that I am a mortal man
And you will lose your once lovd Tiriel[;] alas how faint I am[!"]

["]Impudent fiend[,"] said Ijim ["]hold thy glib & eloquent tongue[.]
[190] Tiriel is a king & thou the tempter of dark Ijim[.]
Drink of this running broo*k*, & I will bear thee on my shoulders[."]

He drank & Ijim raisd him up & bore him on his shoulders[.]
All day he bore him & when evening drew her solemn curtain
Enterd the gates of Tiriels palac*e*, & stood & calld aloud[:]

[195] ["]Heuxos come forth I here have brought the fiend that troubles Ijim[!]
Look knowst thou ought of this grey bear*d*, or of these blinded eyes[?"]

Heuxos & Lotho ran forth at the sound of Ijims voice
And saw their aged father borne upon his mighty shoulders[.]
Their eloquent tongues were dumb & sweat stood on their trembling limbs[.]
[200] They knew twas vain to strive with Ijim[;] they bowd & silent stood[.]

["]What Heuxos call thy father for I [must *del*] mean to sport to night[.]
This is the hypocrite that sometimes roars a dreadful lion[.]
Then I have rent his limbs & left him rotting in the forest
For birds to eat but I have scarce departed from the place
[205] But like a tyger he would come & so I rent him too[.]
Then like a river he would seek to drown me in his waves
But soon I buffetted the torrent[;] anon like to a cloud
Fraught with the swords of lightnin*g*, but I bravd the vengeance too[.]
Then he would creep like a bright serpent till around my neck
[210] While I was Sleeping he would twine[;] I squeezd his poisnous soul[.]
Then like a toad or like a new*t* would whisper in my ears
Or like a rock stood in my wa*y*, or like a poisnous shrub[.]
At last I caught him in the form of Tiriel blind & old
And so Ill keep him[;] fetch your father fetch forth Myratana[."]

[215] They stood confounde*d*, and Thus Tiriel raisd his silver voice[:]

["]Serpents not sons [you see *word illeg* your father *del*]
why do you stand[?] fetch hither Tiriel[!]

75

[*Page 8*]

A little rest I crave a little water from a brook
Or I shall soon discover that I am a mortal man
And you will lose your once lovd Tiriel alas how faint I am

Impudent fiend said Ijim hold thy glib & eloquent tongue
Tiriel is a king & thou the tempter of dark Ijim
Drink of this running brook. & I will bear thee on my shoulders

He drank & Ijim raisd him up & bore him on his shoulders
All day he bore him & when evening drew her solemn curtain
Enterd the gates of Tiriels palace. & stood & calld aloud

Heuxos come forth I here have brought the fiend that troubles Ijim
Look knowst thou ought of this grey beard. or of these blinded eyes

Heuxos & Lotho ran forth at the sound of Ijims voice
And saw their aged father borne upon his mighty shoulders
Their eloquent tongues were dumb & sweat stood on their trembling limbs
They knew twas vain to strive with Ijim they bowd & silent stood

What Heuxos call thy father for I mean to sport to night
This is the hypocrite that sometimes roars a dreadful lion
Then I have rent his limbs & left him rotting on the forest
For birds to eat but I have scarce departed from the place
But like a tyger he would come & so I rent him too
Then like a river he would seek to drown me in his waves
But soon I buffitted the torrent anon like to a cloud
Fraught with the swords of lightning. but I bravd the vengeance too
Then he would creep like a bright serpent till around my neck
While I was sleeping he would turne I squeezd his poisnous soul
Then like a toad or like a newt. would whisper in my ears
Or like a rock stood in my way. or like a poisnous shrub
At last I caught him in the form of Tiriel blind & old
And so Ill keep him fetch your father fetch forth Myratana

They stood confounded. and Thus Tiriel raisd his silver voice

Serpents not sons ~~~~~~~~~~~~~~~~~~~~
                        why do you stand fetch hither Tiriel

PLATE XVIII

[Page 9]

Fetch hither Myratana & delight yourselves with scoffs
For poor blind Tiriel is returnd & this much[?] injurd head
Is ready for your bitter taunts. Come forth sons of the curse[!"]

[220] Mean time the other sons of Tiriel ran around their father[.]
Confounded at the terrible strength of Ijim they knew twas vain[;]
Both spear & shield were useless & the coat of iron mail
When Ijim stretchd his mighty arm. *T*he arrow from his limbs
Rebounded & the piercing sword broke on his naked [limbs *del*] flesh[.]

[225] [Then Ijim said Lotho Clithyma(?). Makuth fetch your father
[Why do you stand confounded thus. Heuxos why art thou Silent

[O noble Ijim thou hast brought our father to (the gates *del*) our eyes
[That we may tremble & repent before thy mighty knees
[O we are but the slaves of Fortune. & that most cruel man
[230] [Desires our deaths. O Ijim (tis one whose aged tongue
[(Decieve the noble & *word illeg; all del*) if the eloquent voice of Tiriel
[Hath workd our ruin we submit nor strive against stern fate

[He spoke & kneeld upon his knee. Then Ijim on the pavement
[Set aged Tiriel. in deep thought whether these things were so
                    These ten lines deleted with five vertical strokes.]

[235] ["]Then is it true Heuxos that thou hast turnd thy aged parent
To be the sport of wintry wind*s* ?["] (said Ijim) ["] is this tru*e*?
It is a lie & I am [tormented(?) *del*] like the tree torn by the wind[.]
Thou eyeless fien*d* & you dissemblers. Is this Tiriels house[?]
It is as false & [*for* as] Math*a* & as dark as vacant[?] Orcus[.]
[240] Escape ye fiends for Ijim will not lift his hand against ye[."]

So saying, Ijim gloomy turnd his back & silent sought
The [gloom *del*] secret forests & all night wanderd in desolate ways

[*Page 9*]

Fetch hither Myratana & delight yourselves with scoffs
For poor blind Tiriel is returnd & this much injurd head
Is ready for your bitter taunts. come forth sons of the curse

Mean time the other sons of Tiriel ran around their father
Confounded at the terrible strength of Ijim they knew twas vain
Both spear & shield were useless & the coat of iron mail
When Ijim stretchd his mighty arm. the arrow from his limbs
Rebounded & the piercing sword broke on his naked ~~body~~ flesh

Then Ijim said Lotho ~~&~~ Clithyma. Makuth fetch your father
Why do you stand confounded thus. Heuxos why art thou silent

Oneble Ijim thou hast brought our father to ~~~~ our eyes
That we may tremble & repent before thy mighty ~~knees~~
Owe are but the slaves of Fortune & that most cruel man
Desires our deaths. O Ijim ~~~~
~~~~ if the eloquent voice of Tiriel
Hath workd our ruin we submit nor strive against stern fate

He spoke & kneeld upon his knee. Then Ijim on the pavement
Set aged Tiriel. in deep thought whether these things were so

Then is it true Heuxos that thou hast turnd thy aged parent
To be the sport of wintry winds. (said Ijim) is this true.
It is a lie & I am ~~like~~ ~~~~ the tree torn by the wind
Thou eyeless fiend. & you dissemblers. Is this Tiriels house
It is as false as ~~Matha~~. & as dark as vacant Orcus
Escape ye fiends for Ijim will not lift his hand against ye

So saying. Ijim gloomy turnd his back & silent sought
The ~~~~ secret forests & all night wanderd in desolate ways

PLATE XIX

78

And aged Tiriel stood & said ["]where does the thunder sleep[?]
Where doth he hide his terrible head & his swift & fiery daughters[?]
[245] Where do they shroud their fiery wings & the terrors of their hair[?]
Earth thus I stamp thy bosom[;] rouse the earthquake from his den
[Display thy *del*] To raise his dark & burning visage thro the cleaving
[world *del*] ground

To thrust these towers with his shoulders. *L*et his fiery dogs
Rise from the center belching flames & roaring*s*, dark smoke[.]
[250] Where art thou Pestilence that bathest in fogs & standing lakes[?]
Rise up thy sluggish limb*s*, & let the loathsomest of poisons
Drop from thy garments as thou walkest wrapt in yellow clouds[.]
Here take thy seat in this wide court. *L*et it be strown with dead
And sit & smile upon these cursed sons of Tiriel[.]
[255] Thunder & fire & pestilen*c*e, here [*for* hear] you not Tiriels curse[?"]

He ceast[;] the heaving clouds confusd rolld round the lofty towers
Discharging their enormous voices. At the fathers curse
The earth trembled[,] fires belched from the yawning clefts
And when the shaking ceast a fog possesst the accursed clime[.]

[260] The cry was great in Tiriels palace[;] his five daughters ran
And caught him by the garments weeping with cries of bitter woe[.]

["]Aye now you feel the curse[,] you cr*y*, but may all ears be deaf
As Tiriels & all eyes as blind as Tiriels to your woes[.]
May never stars shine on your roofs[;] may never [plea(*?*) *del*] sun nor moon
[265] Visit you but eternal fogs hover around your walls[.]
Hela my youngest daughter you shall lead me from this place
And let the curse fall on the rest & wrap them up together[."]

He ceast & Hela led her father from the noisom place[.]
In haste they fled while all the sons & daughters of Tiriel
[270] Chaind in thick darkness utterd cries of mourning all the night
And in the morning Lo an hundred men in ghastly death[.]
The four daughters [& all the children in their silent beds
[*words illeg; all del*] stretchd on the marble pavement silent all
[And *del*] falln by the pestilence[,] the rest moped round in [ghastly fe *del*]
guilty fears
[275] And all the children in their beds were cut off in one night[.]
Thirty of Tiriels sons remain*d*, to wither in the palace
Desolat*e*, Loathe*d*, Dumb [Con *del*] Astonishd waiting for black death[.]

5

And aged Tiriel stood & said where does the thunder sleep
Where doth he hide his terrible head & his swift & fiery daughters
Where do they shroud their fiery wings & the terrors of their hair
Earth thus I stamp thy bosom rouse the earthquake from his den
To raise his dark & burning visage thro the cleaving ground
To thrust these towers with his shoulders. let his fiery dogs
Rise from the center belching flames & roarings, dark smoke
Where art thou Pestilence that bathest in fogs & standing lakes
Rise up thy sluggish limbs & let the loathsomest of poisons
Drop from thy garments as thou walkest wrapt in yellow clouds
Here take thy seat in this wide court let it be strown with dead
And sit & smile upon these cursed sons of Tiriel
Thunder & fire & pestilence here you not Tiriels curse

He ceast the heavy clouds confusd rolld round the lofty towers
Discharging their enormous voices, at the fathers curse
The earth trembled fires belched from the yawning clefts
And when the shaking ceast a fog possest the accursed clime

The cry was great in Tiriels palace his five daughters ran
And caught him by the garments weeping with cries of bitter woe

Aye now you feel the curse you cry. but may all ears be deaf
As Tiriels & all eyes as blind as Tiriels to your woes
May never stars shine on your roofs may never sun nor moon
Visit you but eternal fogs hover around your walls
Hela my youngest daughter you shall lead me from this place
And let the curse fall on the rest & wrap them up together

He ceast & Hela led her father from the noisom place
In haste they fled while all the sons & daughters of Tiriel
Chaind in thick darkness utterd cries of mourning all the night
And in the morning lo an hundred men in ghastly death
The four daughters stretchd on the marble pavement silent all
falln by the pestilence the rest moped round in guilty fears
And all the children in their beds were cut off in one night
Thirty of Tiriels sons remaind. to wither in the palace
Desolate. Loathed. Dumb Astonishd waiting for black death

PLATE XX

And Hela led her father thro the silent of the night
Astonishd silen*t*, till the morning beams began to spring[.]

[280] ["]Now Hela I can go with pleasure & dwell with Har & Heva[,]
Now that the curse shall clean devour all those guilty sons[.]
This is the right & ready way[,] I know it by the sound
That our feet make. Remember Hela I have savd thee from death[.]
Then be obedient to thy father for the curse is taken off thee[.]
[285] I dwelt with Myratana five years in the desolate rock
And all that time we waited for the fire to fall from heaven
Or for the torrents of the sea to overwhelm you all
But now my wife is dead & all the time of grace is past
You see the parents curse. Now lead me where I have commanded[."]

[290] ["]O Leagued with evil spirits thou accursed man of sin[!]
True I was born thy [child *del*] slave[;] who askd thee to save me from death[?]
Twas for thy self thou cruel man because thou wantest eyes[."]

["]True Hela this is the desert of all those cruel ones[.]
Is Tiriel cruel[?] *L*ook. *H*is daughter & his youngest daughter
[295] Laughs at affection[,] glories in rebellio*n*, scoffs at Love!
I have not eat these two days[;] lead me to Har & Hevas tent
Or I will wrap the[*e*] up in such a terrible fathers curse
That thou shalt feel worms in thy marrow creeping thro thy bones
Yet thou shalt lead me. Lead me I command to Har & Heva[."]

[300] ["]O cruel O destroyer O consumer O avenger[!]
To Har & Heva I will lead thee[;] then would that they would curse[.]
Then would they curse as thou has*t* cursd but they are not like thee[.]
O they are hol*y* & forgiving[,] filld with loving mercy
Forgetting the offences of their most rebellious children
[305] Or else thou wouldest not have livd to curse thy helpless children[."]

["]Look on my eyes Hela & see for thou hast eyes to see
The tears swell from my stony fountains. *W*herefore do I weep[?]
Wherefore from my blind orbs art thou not siezd with poisnous stings[?]
Laugh serpent youngest venomous reptile of the flesh of Tiriel[.]

And Hela led her father thro the silent of the night
Astonishd silent till the morning beams began to spring

Now Hela I can go with pleasure & dwell with Har & Heva
Now that the curse shall clean devour all those guilty sons
This is the right & ready way I know it by the sound
That our feet make. Remember Hela I have savd thee from death
Then be obedient to thy father for the curse is taken off thee
I dwelt with Mnratana five years in the desolate rock
And all that time we waited for the fire to fall from heaven
Or for the torrents of the sea to overwhelm you all
But now my wife is dead & all the time of grace is past
You see the parents curse. Now lead me where I have commanded

O cursed with evil spirits thou accursed man of sin
True I was born thy slave who askd thee to save me from death
Twas for thy self thou cruel man because thou wantest eyes

True Hela this is the desert of all those cruel ones
Is Tiriel cruel look. his daughters & his youngest daughter
Laughs at affection glories in rebellion. scoffs at Love!
I have not eat these two days lead me to Har & Hevas tent
Or I will wrap thee up in such a terrible fathers curse
That thou shalt feel worms in thy marrow creeping thro thy bones
Yet thou shalt lead me. Lead me I command to Har & Heva

O cruel O destroyer O consumer O avenger
To Har & Heva I will lead thee then would that they would curse
Then would they curse as thou hast cursed but they are not like thee
O they are holy. & forgiving filled with loving mercy
Forgetting the offences of their most rebellious children
Or else thou wouldst not have livd to curse thy helpless children

Look on my eyes Hela & see for thou hast eyes to see
The tears swell from my stony fountains. wherefore do I weep
Wherefore from my blind orbs art thou not seizd with poisonous stings
Laugh serpent youngest venomous reptile of the flesh of Tiriel

PLATE XXI

[*Page 12*]

[310] Laug*h*, for thy father Tiriel shall give the[*e*] cause to laugh
Unless thou lead me to the tent of Har child of the curse[."]

["]Silence thy evil tongue thou murderer of thy helpless children[.]
I lead thee to the tent of Har[,] not that I mind thy curse
But that I feel they will curse thee & hang upon thy bones
[315] Fell shaking agonie*s* & in each wrinkle of that face
Plant worms of death to feast upon the tongue of terrible curses[."]

["]Hela my daughter listen. *T*hou [child(*?*) *del*] art the daughter of Tiriel[.]
Thy father calls. Thy father lifts his hand into the [air *del*] heavens
For thou hast laughed at my tear*s* & curst thy aged father[.]
[320] Let snakes rise from thy bedded locks & laugh among thy curls[."]

He ceast[;] her dark hair upright stood while snakes infolded round
Her madding brows. *H*er shrieks appalld the soul of Tiriel[.]

["]What have I done Hela my daughter[?] *F*earst thou now the curse
Or wherefore dost thou cry[?] Ah wretch to curse thy aged father[!]
[325] Lead me to Har & Heva & the curse of Tiriel
Shall fail. If thou refuse howl in the desolate mountains[."]

[Page 12]

Laugh. for thy father Tiriel shall give thee cause to laugh
Unless thou lead me to the tent of Har child of the curse

Silence thy evil tongue thou murderer of thy helpless children
I lead thee to the tent of Har not that I mind thy curse
But that I feel they will curse thee & hang upon thy bones
Fell shaking agonies, & in each wrinkle of that face
Plant worms of death to feast upon the tongue of terrible curses

Hela my daughter listen, thou art the daughter of Tiriel
Thy father calls. Thy father lifts his hand into the heavens
For thou hast laughed at my tears, & curst thy aged father
Let snakes rise from thy bedded locks & laugh among thy curls

He ceast her dark hair upright stood while snakes infolded round
Her madding brows. her shrieks appalld the soul of Tiriel

What have I done Hela my daughter feard thou now the curse
Or wherefore dost thou cry Ah wretch to curse thy aged father
Lead me to Har & Heva & the curse of Tiriel
Shall fail. If thou refuse howl in the desolate mountains

PLATE XXII

84

She howling led him over mountains & thro frighted vales
Till to the caves of Zazel they approachd at even tide[.]

Forth from their caves [the sons of Zazel *del*] old Zazel & his sons ran [& *del*]
                                                 when they saw
[330] Their tyrant prince blind & his daughter howling & leading him[.]

They laughd & mocked[;] some threw dirt & stones as they passd by
But when Tiriel turnd around & raisd his awful voice
[They *del*] Some fled away [& hid themselves *del*] but [some *del*] Zazel stood
                                   still & thus [scoffing *del*] begun[:]
["]Bald tyrant. Wrinkled cunning [wretch *del*] listen to Zazels chains[.]
[335] Twas thou that chaind thy brother Zazel[.] *W*here are now thine eyes[?]
Shout beautiful daughter of Tiriel. *T*hou singest a sweet song[!]
Where are you goin*g*? *C*ome & eat some roots & drink some water[.]
Thy crown is bald old man[;] the sun will dry thy brains away
And thou wilt be as foolish as thy foolish brother Zazel[."]

[340] The blind man hear*d* & smote his breast & trembling passed on[.]
They threw dirt after the*m*, till to the covert of a wood
[They *del*] The howling maiden led her father where wild beasts resort
Hoping to end her [life *del*] woe*s*, but from her cries the tygers fled[.]
All night they wanderd thro the wood & when the sun arose
[345] They enterd on the mountains of Har[;] at Noon the happy tents
Were frighted by the dismal cries of Hela on the mountains

But Har & Heva slept fearless as babe*s* on loving breasts[.]
Mnetha awoke[;] she ran & stood at the tent door [in *del*] & saw
The aged wanderer led towards the tents[;] she took her bow
[350] And chose her arrows[,] then advancd to meet the terrible pair[.]

7

In howling led him over mountains & thro fightid vales
Till to the caves of Zazel they approachd at even tide
                              old Zazel & his sons
Forth from their caves ~~~~~~~~~~~~~ ray. ~ when they saw
Their tyrant prince blind & his daughter howling & leading him
They laughd & mockd some threw dirt & stones as they passd by
But when Tiriel turnd around & raisd his awful voice
Some fled away ~~~~~~~~~~~ but some stood still & thus ~~~~ began
                              Zazel

Bald tyrant. Wrinkled cunning ~~~~~ listen to Zazels chains
Twas thou that chaind thy brother Zazel where are now thine eyes
Shout beautiful daughter of Tiriel. thou singest a sweet song
Where are you going. come & eat some roots & drink some water
Thy crown is bald old man. the sun will dry thy brains. away
And thou wilt be as foolish as thy foolish brother Zazel

The blind man heard. & smote his breast & trembling passed on
They threw dirt after them. till to the covert of a wood
The howling maiden led her father where wild beasts resort
Hoping to end her woes. but from her cries the tygers fled
All night they wanderd thro the wood & when the sun arose
They entered on the mountains of Har at noon the happy tents
Were frightid by the dismal cries of Hela on the mountains

But Har & Heva slept fearless as babes. on loving breasts
Mnetha awoke she ran & stood at the tent door & saw
The aged wanderer led towards the tents she took her bow
And chose her arrows then advanced to meet the terrible pair

PLATE XXIII

[Page 14]

And Mnetha hasted & met them at the gate of the lower garden[.]

["]Stand still or from my bow recieve a sharp & winged death[."]

Then Tiriel stoo*d*, saying ["]what soft voice threatens such bitter things[?]
Lead me to Har & Heva[.] I am Tiriel King of the west[!"]

[355] And Mnetha led them to the tent of Ha*r*, and Har & Heva
Ran to the door. *W*hen Tiriel felt the ankles of aged Har
He sai*d*, ["]O weak mistaken father of a lawless race[,]
Thy laws O Har & Tiriels wisdom end together in a curse[.]
[Thy God of Love thy heavens of joy *all del*]
[360] Why is one law given to the lion & the [Ox *del*] patient Ox[?]
[Dost thou not see that men cannot be formed all alike *all del*]
And why men bound beneath the heavens in a reptile form[,]
A worm of sixty winters creeping on the dusky ground[?]
[Some nostrild wide breathing out blood. Some close shut up
[365] [In silent deceit. poisons inhaling from the morning rose
[With daggers hid beneath their lips & poison in their tongue
[Or eyed with little sparks of Hell or with infernal brands
[Flinging flames of discontent & plagues of dark despair
[Or those whose mouths are graves whose teeth the gates of eternal death
[370] [Can wisdom be put in a silver rod or love in a golden bowl
[Is the son of a king warmed without wool or does he cry with a voice
[Of thunder does he look upon the sun & laugh or stretch
[His little hands into the depths of the sea to bring forth
[The deadly cunning of the scaly tribe (flatterer[?] *del*) & spread it to the morning
These eleven lines were each deleted individually.]
[375] The child springs from the womb. *T*he father ready stands to form
The infant head while the mother idle plays with her dog on her couch[.]
The young bosom is cold for lack of mothers nourishment & milk
Is cut off from the weeping mouth with difficulty & pain[.]
The little lids are lifted & the little nostrils opend[.]
[380] The father forms a whip to rouze the sluggish senses to act
And scourges off all youthful fancies from the newborn man[.]
Then walks the weak infant in sorrow compelld to number footsteps
Upon the san*d*, &*c*
And when the [foolish crawling *del*] drone has reachd his crawling length
[385] Black berries appear that poison all around him. Such [is *del*] was Tiriel[,]
[Hypocrisy the idiots wisdom & the wise mans folly *all del*]

8

And Mnetha hastd & met them at the gate of the lower garden

Stand still or from my bow recieve a sharp & wingd death

Then Tiriel stood. saying what soft voice threatens such bitter things

Lead me to Har & Heva I am Tiriel King of the west

And Mnetha led them to the tent of Har. and Har & Heva
Ran to the door. when Tiriel felt the ankles of aged Har
He said. O weak mistaken father of a lawless race
Thy laws O Har & Tiriels wisdom end together in a curse

~~Why is this thing the cause of joy~~

Why is one law given to the lion & the ~~ox the~~ patient Ox

~~that they may not be the cause of joy~~

Some nostrils wide breathing out blood. Some close shut up
In silent deceit. poisons inhaled from the morning rose
With daggers hid beneath their lips & poison in their tongue
Or eyes with little sparks of Hell or with ~~infernal brands~~
Flashing flames of ~~discontent & plagues of dark despair~~
Or those whose mouths are graves whose teeth the gates of eternal death
Can wisdom be put in a silver rod or love in a golden bowl
Is the son of a king warmed without wool or does he cry with a voice
Of thunder does he look upon the sun & laugh or stretch
His little hands into the depths of the sea to bring forth
The deadly cunning of the ~~flattering~~ & spread it to the morning
The child springs from the womb. the father ready stands to form
The infant head while the mother idle plays with her dog on her couch
The young bosom is cold for lack of mothers nourishment & milk
Is cut off from the weeping mouth with difficulty & pain
The little lids are lifted & the little nostrils opend
The father forms a whip to rouze the sluggish senses to act
And scourges off all youthful fancies from the new born man
And when the ~~~~ drone has reachd his crawling length
Black berries appear that poison all around him. Such was Tiriel

And why men bound beneath
the heavens in a reptile form
A worm of sixty winters
creeping on the dusky ground

Then walks the weak infant in
sorrow compelld to number
footsteps
Upon the sand. &

~~Appearing the ————— ————— —————————fully~~

PLATE XXIV

88

[Page 15]

Compelld to pray repugnant & to handle the immortal spirit
Till I am subtil as a serpent in a paradise
Consuming all both flowers & fruits insects & warbling birds
[390] And now my paradise is falln & a drear sandy plain
Returns my thirsty hissings in a curse on thee O Har
Mistaken father of a lawless race my voice is past[."]

[393] He ceast outstretchd at Har & Hevas feet in awful death[.]

[The End]

[Page 15]

Compelld to pray repugnant & to handle the immortal spirit
Till I am subtil as a serpent in a paradise
Consuming all both flowers & fruits insects & warbling birds
And now my paradise is falln & a drear sandy plain
Returns my thirsty hissings in a curse on thee O Har
Mistaken father of a lawless race my voice is past

He ceast outstretchd at Har & Hevas feet in awful death

PLATE XXV

TEXTUAL NOTES

Lines 19–20	The first design shows Tiriel supporting Myratana.
Line 20	Erdman reads: 'living *1st reading del*; ? shriecking, *2nd reading del*'.
Lines 59–60	The second drawing, of Har and Heva bathing, may refer to these lines.
Lines 75–85	The third design, which shows Har, Heva, and Mnetha kneeling on a bed as Har talks to Mnetha, probably alludes to these lines.
Lines 84–86	The fourth design shows Tiriel kneeling before Har, while Heva clutches Mnetha behind Har.
Line 123	The drawing (no. 5) of Har and Heva playing harps may refer to this line.
Line 151	The sixth design represents Har and Heva watching Tiriel's departure.
Lines 167–8	These lines are written in the right margin after line 166.
Lines 192–233	The seventh drawing shows Tiriel on Ijim's shoulders cursing his children.
Line 216	Gleckner and Erdman read the illegible part of the deletion as 'and know'.
Line 237	Gleckner reads the deletion uncertainly as 'torn like'.
Line 244	The 's' of 'daughters' is mended from an accidental 'd'.
Lines 246–9	Elements of this metaphor appear in *Vala*, p. 91:

> when the Earthquake rouzes from his den his shoulders huge
> Appear above the crumbling Mountain. Silence waits around him
> A moment then astounding horror belches from the Centre
> The fiery dogs arise the shoulders huge appear[.]

Lines 257–61	Tiriel beseeched by his children is shown in the eighth design.
Line 264	For 'plea' Erdman reads 'slee[p]'.
Line 266	Here and in *Lines 277, 280, and 283* the 'e' of 'Hela' is faulty, as if it were an 'a' which has been written over. (Gleckner reads questioningly 'Hili'.) Thereafter, in ll. 293, 306, 317, 323, 346, the 'Hela' is quite plain.
Lines 271–7	The death of Tiriel's sons is shown in the ninth design.
Lines 321–7	Hela, with snakes in her hair, leads Tiriel in the tenth design.
Line 326	The original word 'fall' has been converted to 'fail' by erasing the top of the first 'l'.
Lines 347–8	Har and Heva asleep under the care of Mnetha are shown in drawing no. 11.
From line 355	to the end of the manuscript Blake used a sharper pen. It has been suggested, on little evidence, that what follows was written at a later date.

Line 360   This line reappears in a somewhat different form under a picture of Nebu-
                  chadnezzar on Plate 24 of *The Marriage of Heaven and Hell*: 'One Law for
                  the Lion & Ox is Oppression'. See also *Visions of the Daughters of Albion*,
                  Plate 7: 'And is there not one law for both the lion and the ox?'

Lines 362–3   These lines are written in the margin as a continuation of line 361.

Line 370   This line reappears in *Thel* Plate 1 as part of 'THEL's Motto': 'Can Wis-
                  dom be put in a silver rod? / Or Love in a golden bowl?'

Lines 382–3   These lines are written in the right margin at the end of line 381, with an
                  angle bracket to show where they should come in.

Line 393   The last drawing shows Tiriel dead at Hela's feet.

INDEX

PRINTED IN GREAT BRITAIN
AT THE UNIVERSITY PRESS, OXFORD
BY VIVIAN RIDLER
PRINTER TO THE UNIVERSITY